Catamaran Sailing to Win

CHRIS WILSON
and MAX PRESS

Catamaran Sailing to Win

With over 140 photographs and diagrams

Kaye & Ward · London
Hicks, Smith & Sons · Australia & New Zealand
A. S. Barnes & Co · South Brunswick & New York

Acknowledgements

In the compiling of all the details for this book, the photographs and historical data, we were very grateful to have the assistance of many of our friends in the catamaran world. If we were to list the names of all those that have helped us, it would be too lengthy; those that have helped us will know who they are, and to them we offer our sincere thanks.

We must, however, convey our very special thanks to the management and staff of Australia's leading yachting magazine, *Modern Boating*. Without their very comprehensive photographic files and the availability of other reference material, our task would have been much more difficult.

First published in Great Britain 1973
by Kaye & Ward Ltd
21 New Street
London EC2M 4NT

First American edition published 1973
by A. S. Barnes and Company Inc. Cranbury,
New Jersey 08512

Copyright © 1973 Kaye & Ward Ltd

All Rights Reserved. No part of this publication may be reproduced, stored in a retrieval system, or transmitted in any form or by any means, electronic, mechanical, photocopying, recording or otherwise, without the prior permission of the Copyright owner.

ISBN 0 7182 0942 7 (Great Britain)

ISBN 0-498-01392-8 (U.S.A.)
Library of Congress Catalogue Card Number 73-3767 (U.S.A.)

All enquiries and requests relevant to this title should be sent to the publisher and not to the printer.

Printed photolitho in Great Britain by
Ebenezer Baylis and Son Ltd
The Trinity Press, Worcester, and London

Contents

Foreword	7
1 A Decade of Endeavour (History of the Little America's Cup)	9
2 Developing an International C-Class Catamaran	24
3 When You Are All Alone	37
4 Two-Man Cat Teamwork	53
5 'Drifter' Racing Can Be Fun	69
6 Winning in Strong Winds	82
7 Tuning for Faster Sailing	96
8 Gear, Gadgets and Sundry Hardware	121
9 And What of the Future?	145

This book is dedicated to the late Colin Ryrie, who, whilst he never sailed a catamaran, did much to help publicize them through the boating column he wrote in Sydney's *Daily Telegraph* and in his magazine, *Modern Boating*.

Colin's open-mindedness about catamarans, in circles of yachting where much bias once existed, made him a strong ally.

To his memory, and to yachtsmen everywhere, we dedicate this book.

Foreword

When we first became interested in sailing catamarans, in the 1957/58 Australian sailing season, they were very rare, quite unsophisticated, often badly sailed, and openly condemned by sailors of conventional boats. The cats of those days were weird-looking little boats, extremely difficult to tack and with an almost overwhelming desire to trip over their lee bow in strong winds. It was at about this time that the Prout brothers in England and Charlie Cunningham, with his son Lindsay, in Australia created and successfully promoted the first one-design catamaran classes.

And what tremendous development we have seen in fourteen years of catamaran design, sailing and racing. We have seen the introduction of high-aspect ratio rigs, with these rigs getting higher and higher. We have seen the single central centreboard replaced firstly by dagger boards in each hull, and then by swinging centreboards in the hull. We have seen wooden spars replaced by aluminium, and cotton sail cloth replaced by terylene and dacron. And, of course, we now have the trapeze. How did we ever sail a boat well without it?

There has been much development and experimentation in hull construction methods, and this is certain to continue. The moulded fibre-glass bottom with sheet ply topside construction method is in growing use, and we are sure to see a greater use of the very new fibre-glass/end-grain balsa/fibre-glass sandwich method. The new lighter weight techniques of moulding fibre-glass have taken over from moulded plywood, and are now also superseding the 'tortured ply' method. Plywood decking between the hulls was replaced by a netting 'trampoline' and now this has been outdated by the use of heavy-weight sail cloth.

But for all the changes in catamaran design and tuning techniques that we have seen in these years, it is in the rig that the greatest advances have been made. In the mid-sixties we saw the development of the wing mast perfected on boats like *Lady Helmsman* and *Quest II*. The wing masts have since become bigger and bigger... taller, wider and more powerful. On the C-class rig, sophistication is extreme.

Australia's Little America's Cup boat, *Quest III*, has a most intricate system of control battens for regulating sail shape, brilliantly conceived and superbly engineered.

And recently, we have seen the successful development of a total wing sail on a C-class catamaran. The boat carrying this incredible wing sail, *Miss Nylex*, is possibly the fastest boat to windward the world has yet seen. And even on the less sophisticated smaller cats we have seen great progress in rig design. Masts are now bending more and sail shape is more controllable. The loose footed mainsail is now perfected and universally accepted. So too are external wire leech lines, luff downhauls, boom vangs, full width travellers, and other 'go fasts' for downwind.

So now catamarans are sailing much faster. They are much better prepared, and are very highly tuned. And, thankfully, nowadays they are more often very well sailed. No longer are those of us who sail cats looked down on by our fellow mono-hull yachties. Gone are the labels of 'boffin', 'crank', 'extrovert' and other derogatory terms used by the conservative yachtsmen when discussing multi-hulls over an after-race beer.

Yachtsmen the world over now recognize the catamaran as a highly-developed racing sailboat. The International Yacht Racing Union now recognizes three International catamaran classes; the Tornado, Australis and the C-class. We know that the Tornado is enjoying fabulous national racing in many countries throughout the world, with international events of the highest competitive standard. This is sure to continue now that the Tornado has gained Olympic status.

Between us, we have sailed and raced competively in about ten different classes and we have owned or built (or both) more than a dozen boats. Neither of us has yet proved to be a 'world beater' but we have each enjoyed some measure of success in a number of classes. We have been most fortunate in racing in some highly competitive classes with large fleets of first-rate helmsmen. We have also enjoyed racing against and learning from some of the world's leading catamaran sailors, such as Reg White, Bruce Proctor, 'Pom' Mobrand, Ian Fraser, Jörg Spengler, John Osborne, John Weiser, Graham Johnston, Lindsay Cunningham, Maurie Davies, Larry Woods and Dennis Posey.

We certainly treasure our fourteen years of cat racing and cat sailing experience. In the pages of this book we hope that you are able to share with us some of this experience and that you will find your own catamaran sailing more pleasurable and rewarding as a result.

A Decade of Endeavour
(History of the Little America's Cup)

When a group of catamaran enthusiasts on Long Island Sound proposed a match racing series to finally decide which country, the USA or England, had the better boat, John Fisk of Chapmans Sands Sailing Club in England was quick to accept the challenge. Taking the bit between his teeth, Fisk organized for the C-class catamaran *Hellcat II*, with her designer, Rod MacAlpine-Downie as helmsman to begin sailing in England. Fisk teamed with Rod as crew.

The Sea Cliff Yacht Club in New York was enthusiastic about the proposed series and arranged to get a fund under way to finance a trophy. They drafted a Deed of Gift along the lines of the America's Cup system, but for International C-class catamaran racing. This is probably why today the International Catamaran Challenge Trophy is known popularly as the 'Little America's Cup'.

A jeweller designed the rather unattractive trophy which is a set of small silver sails mounted vertically on a black upright cylindrical base.

The first series sailed in 1961 on Long Island Sound was between the British *Hellcat II* and the American *Wildcat*.

The USA defender, *Wildcat*, was chosen from a fleet of several boats available at that time. *Wildcat* was hastily prepared and had not been solidly campaigned.

She started the match against *Hellcat* poorly and was forced to retire in the first two races of the best-of-seven series, thus handing two straight wins to *Hellcat II*. The British were quickly able to capitalize on their early advantage, romping away with the next two races and taking the Cup back to the UK and to Chapman Sands Sailing Club.

The Americans later wrote to Fisk suggesting a return bout for 1962. Fisk replied that the British would be pleased to see another match but that the Americans would have to come to England, as per a clause in the Deed of Gift.

A small fleet of boats assembled on Long Island Sound, and later on Buzzards Bay, to sort out which boat was going to the UK to 'bring back our Cup'. The Bob Harris-designed *Beverly* was chosen and Bill Saltonstall skippered her in the challenge against a hastily prepared *Hellcat I*. This boat was the original MacAlpine-Downie design built two seasons before and had been sold to Ian Norris. Norris was asked to dust her down and race her to defend the Cup.

With Nickie Pope as crew, Norris and *Hellcat* won the first three races, retired in the fourth but came home first in the fifth, easily retaining the Cup. The Thorpe Bay Yacht Club on the Thames Estuary had been asked to run this (and subsequent challenges) as Chapman Sands Sailing Club had neither the facilities nor the membership strength to conduct a successful race series.

Catamaran enthusiasts in Australia had watched the second challenge with much interest and a telegram issuing a challenge from the Australian Catamaran Association was accepted by the British. The 1963 match took place in September

1962. England's Hellcat 1. *The original boat in the Rod MacAlpine-Downie designed series, she was brought out of retirement and sailed by Ian Norris and Nick Pope to defend successfully against the American boat* Beverly. *She looks quite small by today's standard of C-class cat.*

1962. America's challenger Beverly. *Her rather weird looking hulls and raised platform bridge-deck made this Bob Harris design quite outstanding in appearance. Note that the rudder posts are inboard of the transoms.*

off Thorpe Bay after an earnest campaign in Australian waters had seen no less than five new C-class boats built.

(The International Yacht Racing Union had formally adopted the C-class catamaran as an International Class and its limitations were, and still are, LOA 25 feet, BOA 14 feet, maximum measurements, no weight limits, sail area 300 square feet maximum in any form, including spars.)

The Australians raised over eighteen thousand dollars in that year and sent a five-man two-boat team to England where practice sailing took place four weeks before the series to select the ultimate challenger. Skipper John Munns and crew Graeme Anderson chose *Quest* rather than *Matilda*. She was Charlie Cunningham's first C-class. *Matilda*, the other Australian boat, was designed jointly by Peter Joubert and Peter Hooks.

The British defender was the new Mac-Alpine-Downie-designed *Hellcat IIIS*. ('S' for 'Super', they said.) The 1963 match was the first time Reg White skippered the British boat.

The challenge was little short of a disaster for the Australians who, after leading by nearly a mile and a half in the

A DECADE OF ENDEAVOUR

1963. Australia's first C-class cat Southerly. *Based on the hull shape of the* Quickcat, *she never really performed well.*

1963. Australia's first challenger, Quest, *here tuning in Thorpe Bay prior to the match against* Hellcat IIIS. *Skipper John Munns later settled in England as a boat builder.*

first race, had to abandon it for lack of wind. They then lost the next four races after gale-force conditions, more drifters and all sorts of drama had taken place.

Bertie Holloway, who had financed *Hellcat IIIS*, later sold her to the Naval Academy in the USA. This forced the British to get cracking early with a new boat for the 1964 defence against the Americans.

So *Emma Hamilton* was born – a further development of *Hellcat III* with a more sophisticated rig and controls. She became the darling of White's C-class boats, practically vice free, superb to windward, and probably, then, the fastest sailing craft in the world. Named after a fast lady (*Nell Gwynne* was another C-class built that year), *Emma Hamilton* was ready and waiting in plenty of time to meet the Americans.

The Americans had returned to the drawing board but had not spent enough time developing in the sailing arena. Their *Sealion* by the Hubbard brothers was the best C-class yet out of the States – a cat-rigged boat with pretty lines but showing awkwardness in heavy seas that left observers wondering if she would finish a race in that sort of weather.

Holloway took *Emma's* helm, Reg White crewed and they won the first

above: *1963. The second race in the match ended in disaster for the Australians in* Quest. *Fortunately, damage was slight and she completed the series.*

below: *1963.* Matilda, *the other Australian boat that went to Thorpe Bay that year. Many thought her to be the prettiest C built but she was no match for* Quest.

race; *Sealion* won the second; *Emma Hamilton* took the next three straight. The cup didn't even shiver on the British oaken mantelpiece.

Charles Cunningham had been quietly working away on his Quest design in 1964 at Mordialloc, Victoria. With the assistance of a syndicate, he was able to send her to the United States for the World Championship where, with Lindsay Cunningham at the helm and John Buzaglo on the wire, they had all but beaten the pants off the Long Island Sound C-class cats.

Lindsay returned to Australia most impressed with an aerofoil wing mast he had seen. The Cunninghams decided to build a new C-class and *Quest II* was born. Her sloop rig sported a slender aerofoil mast and she walloped the local competition in trials at Blairgowrie, Victoria.

The British again campaigned *Emma*

A DECADE OF ENDEAVOUR

Hamilton but White had included in her wardrobe a flat and smaller mainsail for heavier winds. This challenge turned out to be the most hard-fought so far — a seven-race series. *Quest II* won the first race when the forecast heavy winds did not materialize and *Emma*'s flatter mainsail did not produce enough power. *Quest II*'s three-and-a-half-minute win was devastating against the known best British C-class.

In the next race the British proved they had learnt their lesson. White used the big powerful mainsail instead of the smaller one and began to tune his boat further.

Quest II was losing upwind, but was faster down — much faster. *Emma* passed *Quest* on the final leg after a see-saw fight and won the second race. One all.

Quest was again ahead halfway through the third race when her mast jammed and, in trying to free it, Lindsay Cunningham fell overboard; she lost by only fifty-four seconds. It might as well have been an hour, as this was the race the Australians needed.

Emma came home again in the fourth race after a terrific tactical battle. By now the boats were almost even upwind with *Quest* still slightly superior downwind.

1965. John Munns, who sailed Quest *in 1963, designed and built his own boat,* Joy C, *for the 1965 challenge. His crew has not deserted him! If you look closely you will just be able to see the soles of his feet. He's out very low on the trapeze!*

Quest then rocketed to make it three-all with two good wins.

In the last race, *Quest* was well in the lead — almost three-quarters of a mile, the experts claimed — when out of the locker of Nelson came a forty-five-knot squirt. As White in *Emma Hamilton* was astern, it hit him first. He bore off and rode it downwind. *Quest* was already going full speed downwind when it hit her. She had nothing left to free and she tripped in. *Emma* rode up and past, rounded the last mark and got the gun to keep the Cup.

No one could doubt then that Charles and Lindsay had the finest development in the International C-class, but time does not stand still in design. The Americans were by now again ready to challenge for 1966, having had to sit out in 1965 for the Australians. They chose *Gamecock* as their representative.

A lot of soul searching had been done in Britain after *Quest II* had returned home. They obviously had reached the end of the road with *Emma Hamilton*. Now they had to come up with something which could beat the best the Americans had. They had no doubt heard that *Gamecock* was a goer.

Development work had been going on in the Southampton windtunnel at the University under the direction of Austin Farrer of Seahorse Sails, who had made most of the sails for the British C-class cats and had helped White develop *Emma Hamilton*'s rig. White asked Farrer to work up a rig for a new boat which Helmsman Paints were willing to sponsor. The result was *Lady Helmsman*, a real flier. She was a cat-rigged craft with a huge (by 1966 standards) aerofoil mast.

Bob Shiels and Jim Bonney crewed on *Gamecock* (Shiels is now the USA multi-hull representative on the IYRU). Reg White skippered the Lady again with his brother-in-law, John Osborne, on the wire. *Lady Helmsman* showed that she had not been completely proven — her crew were still learning to set her up and she lost the first race to *Gamecock*.

In the second race *Lady Helmsman* was forced to retire when her mainbeam collapsed under the enormous power exerted by the rig. She was hastily repaired and won the third and fourth races to even the series.

In the fifth, *Gamecock* broke her mainsail halyard lock when sixty seconds astern of the Lady and was forced to retire. In the sixth, *Lady Helmsman* won by only thirty-four seconds, making it UK 4, USA 2, and White's third successful defence. He was named British Yachtsman of the Year for 1966.

Australia again challenged in 1967 with a new cat-rigged boat called *Quest III*, also designed by Charles and Lindsay Cunningham, and crewed by Peter Bolton and Lindsay Rees. *Lady Helmsman* was dusted down and Peter Schneider and Bob Fisher were asked to crew her in the match series as Reg White was too busy. There was a strong feeling in the British camp that the Australians were going to win this challenge. *Quest II* had shown such remarkable ability that the British were sure *Quest III* would be a 'super boat'. But, sadly, this was not the case.

In trials in Australia, *Quest II* had not shown the brilliance of two years before. She was later completely wrecked on Port Phillip Bay. *Quest III* had abandoned the solid aerofoil rig and was trying a wrap-around sock-type arrangement. The boat was virtually a cat-rigged craft with a soft mainsail. *Quest III* was only marginally quicker than a below-par *Quest II*.

In this match, *Quest III* was beaten in every race, except one, when *Lady Helmsman* exploded a centreboard case and had to retire. *Quest III* showed moments of brilliance, especially when reaching hard, but upwind her mast

A DECADE OF ENDEAVOUR 15

1965. Emma Hamilton, the boat that had successfully defended against America's Sealion *the previous year, here trails Australia's* Quest II *to windward.* Quest II *was helmed by co-designer Lindsay Cunningham and was the first wing masted C to compete for the ICCT. Reg White has referred to* Emma *as his sweetest C. Note the bend on the upper section of* Quest's *mast.*

developed a compression S-bend that could not be controlled.

1968 saw the Americans back at Thorpe Bay with *Yankee Flyer*, a new boat sailed by Greer Ellis and Bill Hooten. She sported the old Beverly-style hulls which was surprising considering they were a little out of date. (They were actually new hulls from the old mould.) For the third time, *Lady Helmsman* was dusted down, this time back with the old team, Reg White and John Osborne.

Reg never really liked *Lady Helmsman*. Peter Schneider and Bob Fisher had both called her 'an old cow'. Perhaps her hulls were a little out of date for such a powerful rig.

Yankee Flyer showed promise but she had not been tried and tuned. *Lady Helmsman* won the first race, *Yankee Flyer* the second. A heavier third race saw both boats in trouble. *Lady Helmsman* broke a rudder blade, *Yankee Flyer* had mainsheet problems. *Lady Helmsman* came home over five minutes ahead. She was disqualified in the fourth when she came ashore to change another failing rudder blade. But *Yankee Flyer's* mainbeam broke in the very heavy going and the boat came apart completely. The race was abandoned as spectators raced to salvage the boats. *Yankee Flyer* was sportingly allowed to rebuild and *Lady Helmsman* got herself into top gear in the re-run fourth, this time winning it by sixteen minutes, twenty seconds — a record margin in the history of the event.

The fifth race saw *Yankee Flyer* out for vengeance and she took it by eleven minutes in near windless conditions. The sixth started in twenty-five-knot winds with *Lady Helmsman* finding this to her liking. She had sailed to a two-minute lead when she thumped a big wave and suffered more damage. *Yankee Flyer* caught up and passed the Lady who had broken yet another rudder.

The now repaired *Lady Helmsman* got underway in the next race and passed *Yankee Flyer* to win by over fourteen minutes, making it four to the UK and the Cup as safe as ever.

In 1969, a new nation entered the contest. The Danes came forward and, on this their second attempt to challenge, were accepted by the British. In 1967, Paul Elvstrom had been at Thorpe Bay with *Opus I*, a Danish C-class (in fact, the first Danish C-class) and in short

16   CATAMARAN SAILING TO WIN

1966. USA challenger Gamecock *with Bob Shiels at the helm and Jim Bonney on the wire. The boom is strapped down hard yet twist in the boat still allows the upper leech to fall away.* Gamecock *took two races off the new British defender* Lady Helmsman.

races against *Quest III*, *Opus* had shown she was faster.

Now the Danes set to and designed a new boat they called *Opus III*.

The British realized now that *Lady Helmsman* must be retired. *Yankee Flyer*, had she been properly prepared for all conditions, would probably have won the 1968 challenge. So Reg White pulled out of his factory two hulls from a boat called *Ocelot* which he had tried previously as a C-class. He put the *Lady Helmsman* rig on *Ocelot* to update the boat, but this proved to be her undoing. The hulls were not designed for this powerful aerofoil rig. Nor was the keel line right and the boat was slow to tack.

Opus was well prepared, strong, fast and failure-free. The Danes had not been idle and had studied the previous couple of challenges closely. The Danish skipper was Gert Fredericks and the crew Leif Wagner-Smitt, *Opus III*'s designer.

Ocelot won the close first race by one minute, forty-five seconds. *Opus* won the next, in spite of losing a rudder when she hit a log at over twenty knots.

The Danes were learning to set up their rig, the problem being how full or flat to set the sail. *Ocelot* won the next race by a bare fifteen seconds. The Danes, although well prepared, were losing through lack of big-time race experience. They were forced to retire in the next race. Now it looked all but hopeless for them. But remarkably they came through to win the fifth race by over five and a half minutes. It was Britain's time to fret.

The Danes worked to set their sail better in light airs whilst the British worked to make theirs faster in a blow. The sixth race was a drifter and the Danes completely shattered the British with a twenty-seven-minute win – a new record time, but not unexpected in drifting conditions. The series was tied three-all. Now came the final deciding event. Light

1967. The incredibly powerful British defender, Lady Helmsman *here being beautifully sailed to windward by Peter Schneider and Bob Fisher. Austin Farrer proved in this rig that wing masts were here to stay.*

winds again and the Danes were going faster, yet White and Osborne, from astern, fought every inch of the way to try and avoid defeat. Eventually they were forced to fight the Danes from nearly two laps astern as the Danes prepared to pass them a second time in the same race. The Danes took the Cup, packed up the boat and made off for the land of the Vikings.

America, England and Australia challenged. The Danes accepted the Australian challenge which was mounted by the Sorrento Sailing Club with considerable financial support from Dunlop Australia. *Quest III*, re-rigged with a new light blue aerofoil ply mast, was again campaigned. With Bruce Proctor at the helm and

1967. In the very first race at Thorpe Bay it became apparent that Quest III's *sail could not be controlled. The mainsheet is block-to-block and the leech is falling away very badly. Although seas are only moderate, twist in the boat is apparent.*

Graham Candy on the wire, *Quest III* showed she had the makings of a fast boat in early racing. She was complicated, however, with an incredible amount of gear, wires, levers and systems.

Bill Hollier of Sydney campaigned a boat he and several Botany Bay Catamaran Club members had designed. Called *Red Roo*, she was one of the nicest-looking prospects seen in Australia outside the Quest stable. *Quest III* was chosen and *Red Roo* became her trial horse.

The Danes defended with a new boat called *Sleipner*, helmed by designer-builder Leif Wagner-Smitt and crewed by Klaus Nielsen. Another boat (the one rumoured to have been built for Elvstrom) designed by two SAS pilots-cum-cat enthusiasts, sailed for ten minutes before its unstayed total aerofoil rig broke. This boat showed design brilliance.

Quest III won the first race by one minute, forty-two seconds in twelve to fifteen mph winds. *Quest* then repeated her victory in the second race, and by twelve minutes in the third race. Australia led three-nil. The Danes did some homework and, in the fourth race, were ahead at the final gun. *Quest* had mainsheet problems in that race and again in the fifth. Her complicated gear was starting to misbehave. In fact, with strong, gusty winds looking imminent prior to the start, *Quest* sailed away from the starting line with a jamming mainsheet traveller. *Sleipner* sailed the course alone and when it became obvious that *Quest III* was not able to race, she lowered her mainsail and completed the course under wing mast alone.

In the sixth race, the leveller, the Danes led all the way to win.

Their spirits were up and they were out for victory. This looked like a repetition of the 1969 match. But they had not counted on Jock Sturrock, the Australian team manager. After *Quest III* lost the sixth race and the score was three-all, Sturrock called the Australian camp together for a 'council of war'.

The seventh and final race was a cliff-hanger — very tense for the onlookers. *Quest* won the start, led by thirty-two seconds at the first mark and then applied good covering tactics to hold off the Danes. At the next mark *Sleipner* was just two boat-lengths astern and she closed to

above: *1967. Quest III in her original form had a heavily stayed aluminium mast with 'sock' sail. Although she performed well in trials, her opposition in Australia was mediocre. Peter Bolton took over the helm from Bruce Proctor at short notice, Lindsay Rees crewed.*

left: *1967. James Cook was one of three rather unusual boats built by former Australian team manager, Ron Williams. The wing mast was constructed entirely out of aluminium, the bridgedeck beams were of mild steel tube, and the hulls were glass/foam/glass sandwich.*

five seconds at the close-reaching mark. But the Australians were able to hold off the Danes and win by fifty-six seconds, taking the race, the series and the long-sought-after Cup home to Australia.

With the Cup moving from one hemisphere to another, the change in seasons caused the next match to be delayed until February 1972, when the American challenger, *Weathercock*, met the Australian defender, *Quest III*, off Sorrento in Melbourne. *Quest* had benefited greatly

1970. Off Copenhagen; Quest III, *in the distance, heads the Danish defender,* Sleipner, *upwind. This series was a real cliff-hanger with the Australians taking the Cup by only 56 seconds in race 7.*

1972. Quest III *sails higher and faster than American challenger* Weathercock *soon after the start in race 1.*

A DECADE OF ENDEAVOUR 21

1972. Crew Graham Ainslie come aboard as Bruce Proctor is about to tack Quest III *around the weather mark. The five heavy control battens are clearly visible.* Quest *has twin wind direction indicators on the bows plus four transparent panels with fluttering tape, in the sail.*

from a long and hard-fought series of races in the Australian selection trials in which eight possible defenders lined up. This was the largest C-class fleet ever to take part in a selection series. *Quest III* was the outstanding boat but the talk of the trials was a newcomer, *Miss Nylex*, sporting a full aerofoil rig. In one courageous step, *Miss Nylex*'s designer, Roy Martin, had taken up the challenge of moving straight into the solid wing mast field. *Miss Nylex* proved a wizard boat upwind, but problems of too much power downwind in winds over twenty miles per hour caused her crew to advise selectors that they could not be considered as Cup defenders that year.

Weathercock, George Paterson's creation, was a good boat but *Quest* was easily able to beat her. *Quest* had been raced hard and highly tuned during the selection series. *Weathercock* looked and performed like a C-class cat, three years out of date.

In a dramatic series, which *Quest* won four races to nil, *Weathercock* broke her mast rotating lever in the first race and retired in the second with a broken rudder blade pivot. Then *Quest* got into trouble when her glass and foam bottom began to let gallons of water into her starboard hull. But she was still able to get home ahead in the next two races to win. The Australian skipper, Bruce Proctor, showed more aggression at the start but he was helped tremendously by a brilliant crew, Graham Ainslie, and a good support team ashore led by designer Lindsay Cunningham. Cunningham had reworked the rig and mainsheet systems on the boat. The sail now utilized five main control battens built of flattened aluminium tube in short pieces. These were swivelled on cams so that under tension from a wire set in the tube from the luff to the leech line, they could be made to take up the precise desired shape in the sail. Cunningham

1972. The boat that very nearly defended for Australia, Miss Nylex. *She was remarkably simple with her wing sail being controlled by the skipper with a conventional mainsheet from a central point, and the flap angle controlled by the crew with another sheet. Crew is former* Quest II *wire man, John Buzaglo. At the helm, Chris Wilson.*

also devised swivelling aerofoil section shrouds and forestays which were unique and worked with the rotation of the mast.

There is little doubt that there is a tremendous local advantage for the country holding the Cup. Local enthusiasm is generated with every challenge to build more and more C-class to try to gain the right to defend. Against this, the challenging country has to try to arouse enthusiasm to build one or two boats with which they hope to wrest the Cup away.

Changes in the Deed have been suggested by many C-class enthusiasts for a long time. Ideas like allowing all chal-

A DECADE OF ENDEAVOUR

lenging nations to sail off before the match and the best boat to gain the right to challenge are the most popular so far. Sorrento Sailing Club favours this idea and tried to encourage its adoption for 1972 when they had challenges from England, the USA and Denmark. But they met with no success in gaining acceptance from Sea Cliff Yacht Club in New York, who control the Deed of Gift. A simple answer to the problem is to suggest to Sea Cliff Yacht Club that they surrender the control of the Deed to the holding club and allow that club to administer it as they see fit (just as the New York Yacht Club administers the Deed of Gift for that other famous Cup, whilst they hold it).

Meanwhile, it seems we are to be treated to more and more development in the C-class as ambitious cat enthusiasts try to win or keep the Little America's Cup. In this respect, the International C-class is playing more than a small part in contributing to small boat development throughout the world.

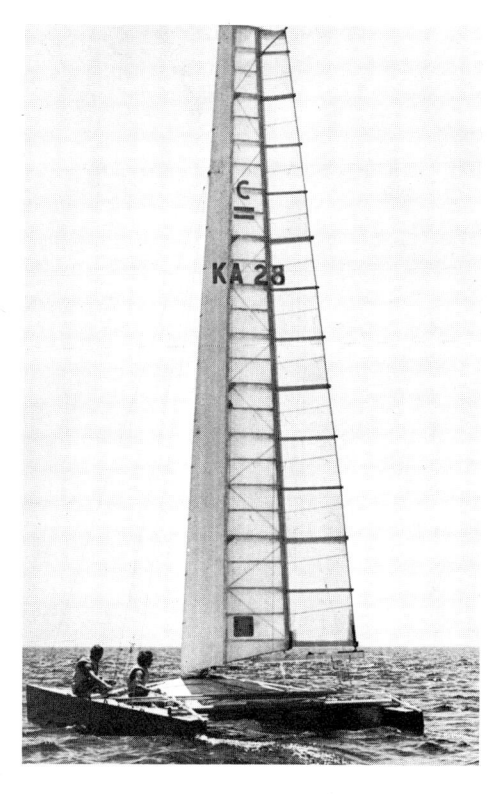

above: *1972. Third best Australian C was* Helios *with hulls designed by the well-known creator of tris, Lock Crowther, and rig by Frank Bethwaite. Skipper and driving force behind the boat was Bill Hollier.* Helios *did show potential but was fraught with highly complex technical problems.*

below: *1972.* Quest III *shows her 'power plus' in fresh wind and smooth sea.*

Developing an International C-Class Catamaran 2

Many cat sailors have at one time or another thought about designing and building a C-class catamaran. The motivation for this is, of course, the Little America's Cup and the honour of possibly representing one's country in the event. Although we believe that many have contemplated tackling a C-class, it is true that relatively few have actually done so.

It can be a mammoth task. It can be fraught with frustration. Often thousands of pounds are involved in developing a boat that is ultimately worth only a fraction of the total cost. Very few C-class designers or builders can claim to have been successful, and rarely is this at their first attempt. But in spite of the problems, the amount of time required, and the cost, C-class cats will continue to be developed because they represent the ultimate in high performance catamaran design. The Little America's Cup will continue to have the most prestige of any catamaran trophy in the world.

We have had varying degrees of involvement in Australia's attempt to win the Little America's Cup. It started back in 1962 when the Australian Catamaran Association first set their sights on gaining the cup for Australia. We have been involved in fund raising, team and boat selection, team management, plus the building and sailing of C-class cats. To date, we have not participated to the extent of actually sailing one of the boats in a match series, but maybe one day . . . !

The interest in the development of new C-class cats certainly does not appear to be waning. In 1972, a total of eight different C-class cats competed for the right to defend the Cup for Australia against the American challenger, *Weathercock*. By far the oldest boat in this fleet was the rather elderly but highly modified *Quest III*. Another boat was an open B-class carrying an enlarged rig, but the other six boats in the fleet were all totally new C-class catamarans. A conservative estimate is that in excess of £15,000 was spent on the six boats, yet none was successful in beating *Quest III*. Some of these boats will again be raced in a modified form and may still have a chance of success. But for most, it is 'back to the drawing board'!

The development of an International C-class cat requires a combination of very special skills. Rarely will one person alone have all these necessary skills, so most boats are the result of a team or syndicate effort. Syndicates vary in size from two (skipper and crew) to seven or eight. But the size of the syndicate is of little importance. What is absolutely critical is, firstly, the desire to succeed, and, secondly, inspirational leadership.

Usually the idea for a C-class cat starts with one person, who in turn influences a number of his friends to take part in the project. The instigator may even approach people having what he believes to be the necessary skills, and invite them to participate. For example, a designer, boat builder or helmsman might be co-opted onto the team. But we believe that unless every person involved in the development of the boat; the building, finishing, sailing and tuning, is

Many problems can be overcome by careful planning. Here Miss Nylex *designer, Roy Martin, discusses rigging systems with syndicate instigator-cum-crew, John Buzaglo. Although the model appears rather crude, they were able to reach conclusions about rotation limitation factors applicable to the full-size rig.*

totally dedicated to the task, it is doomed to failure even before the plans are drawn.

We believe that many potentially great C-class cats have failed because the syndicate behind the boat did not realize the magnitude of the task they were undertaking and they ran out of time, money or enthusiasm. C-class cats will become more complex, more difficult and costly to design and build. It seems that the total wing rig is with us for at least the immediate future, and this creates considerable problems in transporting the boat, hoisting the rig and storing it. This is all the more reason for having a team of enthusiastic helpers behind every boat.

Let us assume that you have a small group of catamaran enthusiasts who are determined to design and build a C-class catamaran to try for the Little America's Cup, and look at how you might go about planning and carrying out the project. We will assume that the group has the drive, determination and will-power to see the task through, and that they have a great deal of spare time, plus very deep pockets.

Basically, there are two ways of going about developing a new C-class catamaran. One is much more difficult and costly than the other. The first way, and the more simple, is to take an existing design and set out to improve on it. The extent of these improvements or modifications will depend on the success of the design that has been chosen. They might be relatively straightforward tuning and rig refinements or quite extensive basic design changes. Either way, the fact that the chosen design has already been tested will help greatly in simplifying the whole project.

The second, and far more complex,

way is to start from scratch and create a boat that is totally new in design. This can involve considerable research and theoretical testing even before the final design is completed. It is costly and very time consuming. It also happens to be the way that is most frequently chosen.

The reason why most C-class cat syndicates choose the more difficult method of starting from scratch is simply explained. It is the nature of the task itself that drives them to attempt to break new ground. A new C-class catamaran is a form of creative expression. The boat represents the best opportunity for a group of dedicated cat enthusiasts to demonstrate their various talents. If they were interested only in making a boat sail faster, they would be content to exercise their minds on one of the international one-design classes such as the Tornado or Australis.

So now you have decided that you will 'do your own thing'. You will design and build a C-class cat that is totally new and you need a group of people who can accomplish this. In other words, you need to form a syndicate. Whether the leader of your syndicate is the designer, helmsman, builder or financier is not important. We would suggest, however, that the better organized syndicates are made up of the following members:
  Designer
  Builder
  Manager
  Helmsman
  plus at least one or two others.

The Designer. Of course, the designer must be the most important member of the group because it is the quality and interpretation of his ideas that will result in success or failure. The designer must determine the overall concept for the boat, even if some of the individual elements are designed by others. He must

Designer Roy Martin looks worried about his wing rig creation. This is the 125 square foot test version that proved to the Miss Nylex *syndicate that a full-size wing could work.*

create the hull shape and rig detail and be totally responsible for controlling the ultimate weight of the boat. He will also need carefully to supervise all aspects of the boat construction and be available for consultation by the builder at short notice. (See page 34 for a summary by the designer of *Miss Nylex*.)

The designer must also be able fully to understand the problems involved in racing a C-class cat so that he can develop control systems that are both practical and reliable. He should also become so totally involved with the boat that he is present whenever it is sailed or raced. All

DEVELOPING AN INTERNATIONAL C-CLASS CAT

Full-size wing mast for Miss Nylex *under construction. The dark-coloured frames are plywood, the light-coloured ones are balsa.*

good designers will have a complete and up-to-date knowledge of all recent developments in C-class and other high-performance classes, and will be familiar with the latest materials, building techniques and general technological advances that may be useful. If you are lucky, he will also be conscious about cost, but unfortunately this is often a designer's Achilles Heel.

The Builder. Sometimes the actual builder of the boat is also a member of the syndicate but this need not necessarily be the case. In fact, quite often more than one builder will be used for various parts of the boat. If, however, the majority of the work is being carried out by one boat builder and he is not involved in building other competitive C-class cats at the same time, it is not a bad idea to make him part of the syndicate. It will give him more than just a commercial interest in the boat, and maybe you will save some money this way too.

The Manager. It is not essential to have as a member of your syndicate a person who holds the title of 'syndicate manager', but it is essential that one

Miss Nylex *was so outstanding in appearance that she created a great deal of interest from the news media. The sponsoring company considered that the news coverage more than repaid their investment in the boat.*

member of the group assumes this responsibility. Of course, it might be the designer, the builder, the helmsman or even the financier who acts as the manager of the syndicate. But whoever it is, he must have the ability to get the best out of the others in the group, to keep the peace and co-ordinate all the various bits and pieces that go together to make a C-class catamaran. He should also be responsible for controlling costs.

The Helmsman. The helmsman may well be one of the three already mentioned and this is quite satisfactory. The important point is that the helmsman should be nominated right at the start of the project and be a part of it all the way. In selecting a helmsman, you should look for someone who has a proven racing record in other high-performance classes, preferably larger cats, and who has shown an ability to adapt quickly when changing from one class to another. A good C-class cat helmsman will also have an inventive flair, particularly in the area of fittings, gear and gadgetry on the boat.

These four, the designer, the builder, the manager, and the helmsman, will form the nucleus of a C-class cat syndicate but it is desirable for more than four to be involved at various stages of construction and sailing. We are not suggesting that you have ten people in your syndicate, for this would be quite chaotic. But it did take a minimum of six people to hoist the wing mast on *Miss Nylex*, and about the same number to lower it. And this had to be done before and after sailing *each* time the boat took to the water! So by all means keep the organizing syndicate to a minimum to avoid long arguments and the inability to make rapid decisions, but try and recruit a group of interested helpers who can be called on at short notice to give assistance.

Having gathered together as a syndicate, obviously the first and most important decision to be made is the basic concept of the boat. At this stage, and throughout the project, you must have complete faith and total confidence in your designer. If you find that you are frequently in conflict with his ideas, then you have the wrong designer. We do not suggest, however, that you give in meekly to his every wish and whim. Not at all. If your designer wants something on the boat that is untried, radical or even con-

DEVELOPING AN INTERNATIONAL C-CLASS CAT

troversial, put him on the spot. Make him explain and justify his ideas. Let him take you through the same thought processes that he has already been through in arriving at his conclusion. Your designer ought to be able to convince you that his way is the right way, and if he cannot, you must begin to doubt his own conviction in the idea. But remember, when the chips are down and there is a decision to be made, it must be the designer who has the final say. And having made the decision, his fellow syndicate members must share his enthusiasm for the idea.

So we now assume that your designer has made a recommendation for a particular type of C-class cat which all the members of the syndicate agree will have the best chance of beating the opposition. The next step is to attempt to determine what it will cost to build the boat. We say *attempt* to establish cost because we have had some experience in trying to estimate the cost of a C-class cat and know just how difficult it can be. We know of one revolutionary Australian boat that cost nearly £4,000 against a budget of £2,250. If you do not have a bottomless pit of money and have to be reasonably close in your cost estimate, we suggest that you look at all the separate components of the boat and put a cost to each of these. For example, the separate items might be:

Hulls.	Mast (and spare).
Beams.	Rigging.
Trampoline.	Control gear.
Centreboards, rudders.	Sails, battens (if any).
Fittings, sheets.	Paint, finishes.
Mast raising gear.	Boat cover.
Spares.	Crew equipment.

When setting a cost for each of these items, we would suggest that you tend to overestimate. It is human nature to underestimate the cost of anything. It is also a good idea to build a reserve figure of at least twenty per cent into your total estimate.

In addition to the cost of the boat itself, there are a few extra costs which often do not occur until the boat is nearing completion. Storage of a C-class cat, particularly one with a wing mast, can be rather difficult, and during the final finishing of the boat it will be important for it to be kept under cover, preferably in a space large enough for it to be assembled and worked on. It could well be necessary to rent premises for this final setting up and storage.

This is the 'magic box' on the base of Miss Nylex's *wing. A terribly complex and ingenious device, it controlled the flap angles while sailing. The four wires disappear through sheaves, ultimately finding their way to the flaps. The ropes move the 'box' around a single axis and lead through cam cleats for the crew to control. The central rope, through a small block, regulates the relative angle of top flap to the lower flap.*

Sometimes they fall down! The wing off Miss Nylex *is taken in tow after the crew had cut it adrift to prevent damage. The mast fell down when the lashing on the side stay parted. (See inset photograph.)*

Just as a C-class cat can be difficult to store, it can also be very difficult to transport from place to place. It is true that the twenty-five-foot hulls and beams can be carried on a trailer behind most cars but a thirty-five to forty-foot by nine-foot wing mast requires a large semi-trailer. You should also examine the merit of insuring your boat. A full cover for transportation, vandalism, theft, sailing and racing will be very costly indeed, because these boats are so susceptible to damage. But it is well worth talking to a few insurance companies to establish whether or not insurance is worth while.

Having established a budget for the boat and allowed a reserve to cover the contingencies, you must of course determine how the boat is to be financed. You may have sufficient funds within the members of the syndicate or you may elect to seek a sponsor. A third and quite common alternative is partly to finance the boat yourselves and seek commercial sponsorship for the remainder. As these intricate and complex sailing machines become more sophisticated and developed, their cost will continue to rise.

So much so that the private financing of new C-class cats will become more difficult and those keen on developing new boats will look more and more for commercial sponsorship.

If your decision is to seek commercial sponsorship, we suggest that you prepare a formal submission in writing to present to prospective sponsor companies. To enable them to evaluate the proposal fairly, it should contain a thorough summary of your plans for the boat, why you think it will be a winner, and what you expect it to cost. Your proposal should also include a run-down on each of the syndicate members, their sailing experience or their qualifications generally. Most commercial sponsors of C-class cats are looking for public relations benefits from their involvement so it may well influence their decision if you are able to accompany your proposal with a collection of press clippings or a scrap book from a previous challenge or selection series.

If you are building a C-class under commercial sponsorship, it is most important for the syndicate controlling the

DEVELOPING AN INTERNATIONAL C-CLASS CAT 31

Appearance is not everything. When Quest III first appeared, her 'sock' sail system looked very efficient. But it proved impossible to control and the boat was a failure with this rig.

An historical shot of Quest III *in her original form shows at a glance why this rig failed. Although being sailed here in quite moderate conditions on Port Phillip Bay, the mast is S-bending alarmingly.*

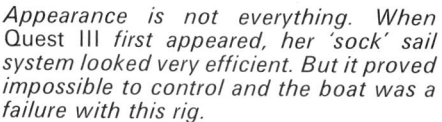

design and construction of the boat to control the funds. Suggest that your sponsor makes lump sum payments of, say, £1,000 a time as required by the syndicate. A special trading bank account can easily be opened to facilitate the control of finances. By operating this way, the boat syndicate will then have the complete freedom to allocate the funds as they see fit without the concern of having 'Big Brother' (the sponsor) looking over their shoulder or questioning their decisions.

So that the sponsor may gain the utmost in public relations benefit from the venture, we suggest you consider naming the boat after your sponsor company or after one of the company's products. Contrary to the belief of many people, this practice is permitted by most national yachting authorities, without running foul of the rule relating to amateurism. But the

left: Quest III's wing mast is directly facing the camera and does not look 3' 7" deep. But this picture shows that wing masts do bend. Quest's wing measured 12" maximum thickness and was 40' 7" tall.

above: The designer, if not one of the two crew, should always be on hand when the boat is being raced to offer advice and to discuss improvements with the crew. Here skipper Bruce Proctor adjusts Quest III's leech line control while Lindsay Cunningham looks on.

conditions under which a company name can be used are quite restrictive and it is wise to seek guidance from your national authority at the time of registering the name.

As a guide only, we have set out below the conditions suggested by the Australian Yachting Federation when registering the name *Miss Nylex*. (*Miss Nylex* is sponsored by the plastics manufacturer, Nylex Corporation Limited.)

1. The crew do not earn their living from yacht racing.
2. The sponsor company has no advertising value from the venture other than a goodwill intention.
3. Trade marks or other forms of advertising do not appear on any part of the boat.
4. The boat, name of the boat or crew are not used in any advertising for the company or for its products.

It is interesting to note that some sort of a precedent has been established already by some national yachting authorities in accepting names such as *Lady Helmsman* (paint), *Miss Senior Service* (cigarettes) and *Black Bottle* (brandy).

One of the most difficult aspects of any C-class building project is the timing, planning and co-ordinating of all the various tasks that go together to make a complete boat. We have witnessed many instances where a boat has not been able to give of her best because of late launching and lack of tuning time before a selection series. It is a common fault to

DEVELOPING AN INTERNATIONAL C-CLASS CAT

Four of Australia's eight C-class on the beach at Sorrento, Victoria, prior to the 1972 selection trials. From left to right they are: Pegasus, Quest III, Gayle *(a sloop rigged* Quest III *type) and* Panther *(a sister ship of* Quest *but carrying a more simple and less effective rig).*

underestimate the amount of time required to complete a particular task, and because many of the tasks in building a C-class cat are experimental or untried, it is even more difficult to be precise about the time needed. So allow plenty of time to complete your boat, and plan on being in the water at least eight weeks before the boat has to be raced seriously. We have seen some boats built using the management planning techniques of PERT and Critical Path Method, yet still be late in the water. On the other hand, we have watched other boats proceed smoothly to a pre-determined plan and be launched in plenty of time for adequate tuning. Hence the importance of having a strong and able manager in a C-class syndicate.

If you are fortunate enough to get sponsorship from a commercial organization, you may become a little concerned that in their attempt to gain publicity for the boat, a breach of security could occur. Not that the design and building of a C-class catamaran can ever be done in complete secrecy, but in the early days of your development there may be some aspects of your boat that you would be happier if the opposition did not know about. On the one hand you will be keen to keep the press away while the boat is being built, yet your sponsor will also be keen to gain some publicity in the early stages, even if it is only for their house magazine. Common sense will ultimately prevail. A compromise is to take a series of photographs during the building that can be used later on, allow the sponsor to publicize the boat when it is about one half completed. At this time it is likely that other boats being built will be too far advanced to gain any advantage from knowing some of the details of your boat.

Launching a C-class cat can be tricky. There are so many little things that need watching and adjusting in getting the boat rigged and into the water that it is impossible for the two-man crew to cope on their own. In our experience it takes at least four people, and preferably five or six, to rig a C-class and manhandle the boat into the water. If you are able to muster the same two or three helpers each time you sail the boat, so much the better. You will then be able to develop a set routine to save time and effort. This is one of the reasons why syndicates of five or six people are best.

What help does the crew need in sailing and tuning a C-class cat? If the boat's designer is not one of the two sailing the boat, he should be present during all the early sailing and racing of the boat. Preferably, he should watch the boat sailing from a fast power boat and be available to make suggestions and discuss problems with the crew after each sail. Also the boat's builder should take an active interest in the early working-up trials, particularly if structural modifications are being considered.

In spite of the relatively high cost involved, the very high risk of failure and frustration, plus the personal sacrifices required to design and build a new C-class catamaran, most people who go through with it agree that the effort has been worth while. Very few cat sailors consider the C-class as their 'usual class'. In almost every case, the fellows sailing in C-class have come from other classes, and look upon their C-class involvement as being only temporary. The mere fact that International C-class has the ability to bring together yachtsmen from a variety of classes and give them a common purpose is almost reason alone for the existence of the class.

We do not believe that regular weekly fleet racing for C-class will ever take place anywhere in the world in the future except in the two countries that are about to meet in a Little America's Cup match series. But that does not reduce the importance of the class in international yachting or in the contribution it can and does make to catamaran design evolution generally. Certainly, the design of a Little America's Cup winner will remain as the ultimate goal for any catamaran designer.

SUMMARY BY A SYNDICATE DESIGNER

The following sketches and summary were prepared by Roy Martin, the designer of the wing-sailed *Miss Nylex*, *before* the syndicate had decided to proceed with a total wing rig. It is one example of a designer having prepared a well-thought-out argument to support his own views and to gain the backing of his fellow syndicate members.

'Proposal (3) is most attractive because of the high possible maximum lift coefficient and small stall angle. Also a high mast rotation angle is possible with the relatively simple four-wire staying system.

'Its greatest drawback is the size of the rigid wing section which may cause unacceptable rigging problems. In predictable fair weather it might be acceptable to leave the mast rigged but under normal conditions it would have to be raised and lowered for overnight storage. For shipment and storage it could be divided at the start of the tapered section. The largest single part would then be 20' × 7' 6" × 1' 3", which is about the size of half the hulls.

'The weight should be acceptable. It is expected that the absence of the high control wire forces will permit lighter weight structures to be used, compared with either proposal (2) or (1). Skinning with thin A.B.S. sheet, used to take some of the loads, might be possible and would give an excellent surface finish at no more than material cost.

'Under the heading of aerodynamic efficiency, proposal (3) has several advantages:
1. Characteristics are built-in and are therefore predictable. With either (1) or (2) the ideal section characteristics may not be achieved because of the difficulties

DEVELOPING AN INTERNATIONAL C-CLASS CAT

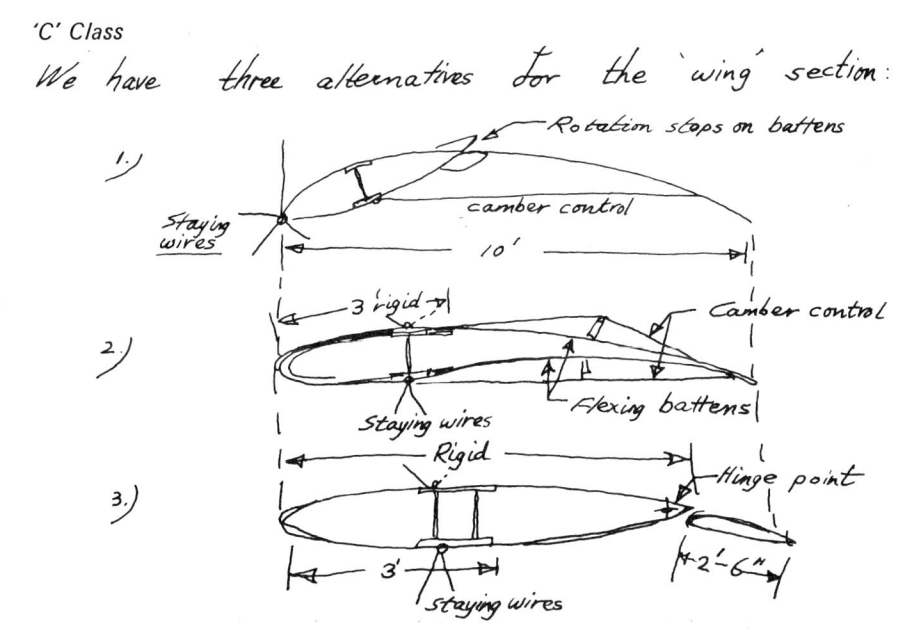

'C' Class

We have three alternatives for the 'wing' section:

1.) [sketch: Rotation stops on battens; camber control; Staying wires; 10']

2.) [sketch: 3' rigid; Camber control; Staying wires; Flexing battens]

3.) [sketch: Rigid; Hinge point; 3'; 2'-6"; staying wires]

The advantages and disadvantages may be tabulated as follows:

	Type 1	Type 2	Type 3
Aerodynamic efficiency	moderate	good	excellent
Ease of construction and repair	OK	OK	OK
Weight	100%	110%	100%
Control forces (camber control)	high	very high	low
Ability of staging to permit mast rotation	difficult	OK ← and wire system → OK	
Ease of turning	difficult	difficult	easy
Ease of control in sailing (camber setting, and gust release)	fair	fair	easy
Ability to achieve very high camber	fair ←	limited by batten elasticity	→ fair	excellent
Maximum lift coefficient/ Stall angle with max. camber	1·6/ 15°–20°	1·6/ 15°–20°	2·5/ 25°–30°
Difficulties in rigging	fairly complex	unproven should be easier than 1	unproven see notes

of tuning the battens to conform to the ideal shape.

2. The finish can be made very smooth over the whole surface with tangible reduction in drag.

3. Rigging wires can be moved back, away from the leading edge where they must create disturbance of the air flow, resulting in drag.

'At the moment, the results of sailing trails indicate that there is a substantial gap between achieved and theoretically possible performances. This can only be explained by efficiency losses from such factors as turbulence at the base of the mast, turbulence caused by rigging wires (not necessarily drag of the wires as such, but the magnified effect on the sail), losses in effective sail area due to the pointed peak, and relatively rough shapes and surfaces.

'It appears from all the theories that much greater accuracy in creating the right section shapes is the most promising area for rig development. But there is little prospect that types (1) and (2) can, in practice, be made to perform as intended without a great deal of tuning on the beach.

'One may get the uncomfortable feeling with a completely rigid wing that there is no room for tuning and that it is a 'do or die' situation. This is in fact true, but the chances of 'doing' are much greater than with a rig which requires tuning on the beach. In normal tuning we simply try to create the theoretically ideal shapes by trial and error, and in most cases the results are far from perfect.

'The rigid section approach imposes on the designer the responsibility of providing the right shape to begin with. Whilst this is a complex problem, the parameters are now sufficiently well defined for a choice to be made which will yield a performance theoretically far superior overall than either a 'conventional' wing mast, or the intermediate double-luff type with full camber control, at the expense of some difficulty in rigging.'

Roy Martin. 5 April 1971

'C' Class:- rigid wing with high lift flap

When You Are All Alone . . .   3

Racing a single-handed catamaran can, in many ways, be much more rewarding than racing the two-man type. The skipper's personal performance in a race, good, bad or indifferent, reflects directly on him; there can be no excuses for there is no one else to blame. It is a very personal experience, sailing alone.

The demands placed on the skills of the helmsman of a single-handed cat require an attitude of single-mindedness to win — a desire to beat the other chap and the rest of the fleet — which can be compared to playing chess or running the hundred-yard sprint. The amount of success and satisfaction gained from a race depends entirely on the effort put into it by the individual. Hence you often find that the single-handed sailor, cat or mono-hull, is a more dedicated yachtsman. He tries harder to be fitter, races harder to win, sails harder to achieve a personal victory, practises more often, and tunes and fiddles more to get the boat into top gear and keep it there.

This personal sort of racing attracts a very special type of yachtsman, and keeps him in it for years. Comradeship is often higher among sailors of single-handed boats than among those sailing other types.

Like most other types of craft, the single-handed cat requires special attention to detail to get the utmost from it. Systems need to be simpler and easier to work than on two-man boats where there are two pairs of hands instead of one. The aim should be to rig the single-hander as simply as possible, yet with every necessary device that will allow instant adjustment. You can learn from watching the top boats in your class. They will have already settled into a certain 'ideal' pattern of devices, systems and gadgets. Often it is better to copy the experts and later work out which system you want to scrap and which you want to retain. Scrapping the systems you do not want can later be followed by the addition of better systems or by devising better ones yourself. But try to keep the boat as simple as possible to keep down unnecessary weight and to help your boat's reliability.

THE SINGLE-HANDED TYPES

There are three basic types of mono-cat. These can be identified by the method of hiking used when racing.

The first is probably the oldest: *no hiking device at all*, apart from foot straps which enable the skipper to lean at least some of his weight outboard.

The second type is the catamaran with a *hiking plank* that slides outboard and on which the skipper can sit to trim his craft.

The third and latest method now becoming universally popular in any new design is *the trapeze*.

The first two methods can require a good deal of physical effort. Hiking outboard from footstraps in strong winds is demanding and often very tiring. The weak eventually give in and sit on the windward gunwale which causes them to drop astern rapidly.

The hiking plank, if it is fixed and does not swivel aft, is quite comfortable and easy to operate, especially upwind. It is

above: *The fleet's away, and from now until the finish it's man against man, boat against boat. In this small fleet of Quickcats, it seems that the boat on the other side of 1458 has won the start. But watch out for 1854 — this boat is being sailed at full speed, driving hard and appears to be pointing a little higher to windward than the rest of the fleet.*

right: *In cat sailing, the Australis represents the ultimate test of single-handed racing. Note the block-to-block situation with the mainsheet which is not good. Luff tension could also be increased.*

usually pulled out to its entire length and the skipper is able to adjust his position to suit the wind strength. Downwind, however, he will need to sit further aft than the plank will permit and make use of footstraps to stop the boat nosediving. This would certainly happen if he stayed on the plank whilst reaching.

The swivelling hiking plank (one that pivots fore and aft as well as sliding in and out) can be used both upwind and down with considerable comfort. It almost makes life too easy. But greater downwind speeds can be achieved because the swivelling plank allows the weight of the skipper to have maximum effect, holding the boat level and the lee bow from diving.

The trapeze, which once was used only on sailing craft with two or more crew, has come into its own on the newer single-handed catamarans. The trapeze allows every position offered by the swivelling plank, and more. The versatility of the trapeze as a hiking device is unquestionable. The one-man crew, clipped onto his trapeze, can be outboard and hiking quicker than the skipper using a plank. The trapeze wire, hooked onto the belt worn by the skipper, takes most of his weight. The skipper's legs can be bent to bring his weight inboard in a lull, and straightened to get his weight quickly outboard to take advantage of a puff. He can move aft as he rounds a windward mark and bears away to go onto a reach. He needs only to adjust the length of his trapeze by means of a small block and tackle to allow him to move aft and keep his body in line with the gunwale without 'shortening' the wire. The trapeze and belt together are lighter than the plank, require little or no maintenance and will be seen on every new single-hander from now on.

Admittedly, getting outboard using a trapeze takes some practice, especially for those who are more familiar with the plank system. It is a technique which must be learned quickly so that you can set about the serious business of racing and not spend time afloat working out

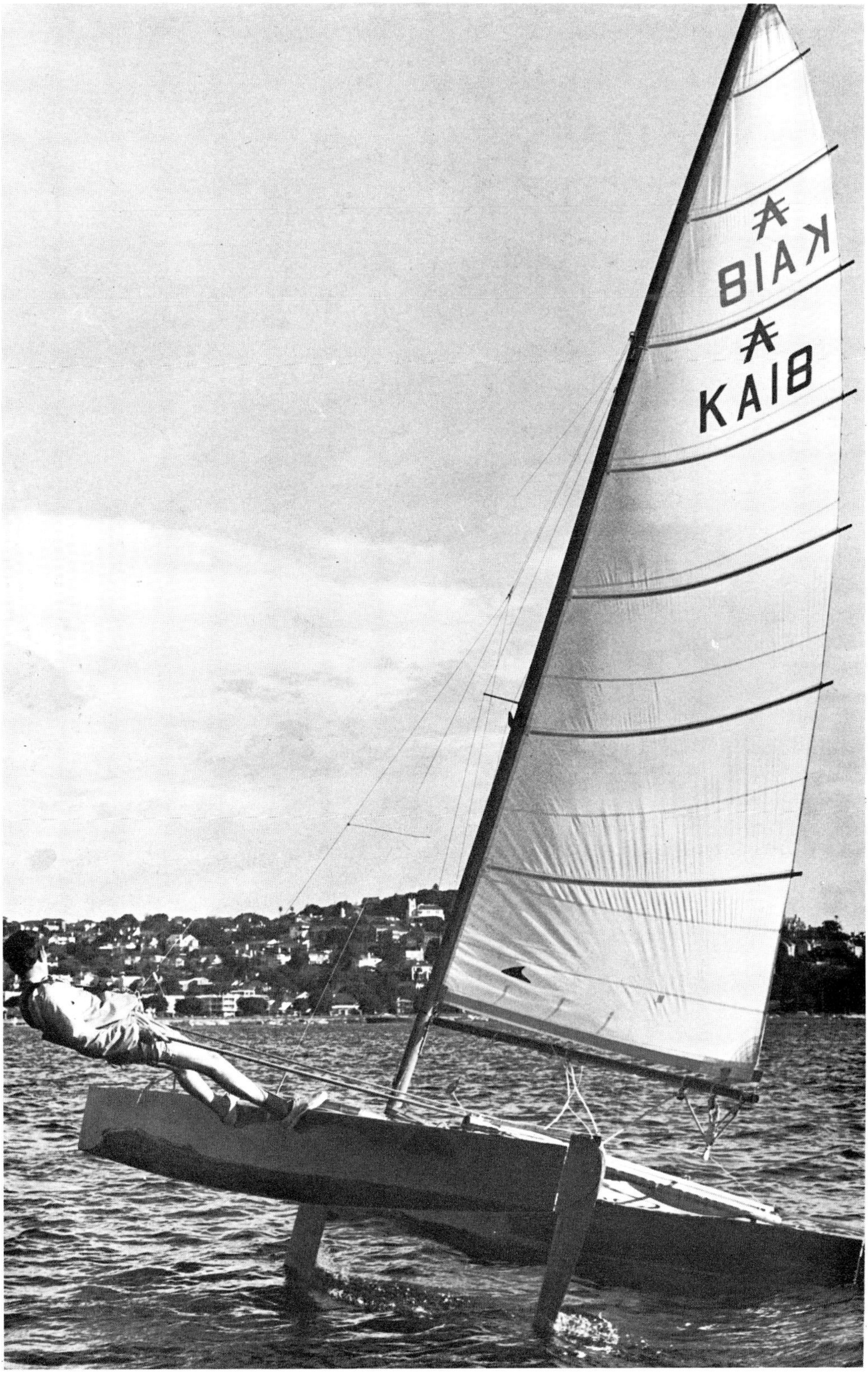
KA18
KA18

CATAMARAN SAILING TO WIN

When the weather centreboard leaves the water, there is too much heel. A boat cannot possibly sail at near maximum speed when at this angle. The skipper should ease the sheet and bear away slightly to make the most of a sudden gust of wind.

even on a proud run, most catamarans, especially the single-hander, achieve a better performance if the crew weight is well forward. The basic rule to apply for downwind racing is to move well forward in light winds, move amidships in moderate winds, and move well aft in heavy winds.

There have been many attempts to develop a trapeze that never needs to be unclipped. On each tack, you would come into the boat, duck across under the boom and swing out on the new windward side. Perhaps this trapeze will be perfected in the near future. If so, it will revolutionize the trapeze for single-handed skippers.

It almost goes without saying that whatever gear you set up on your boat, it must work and it must be simple. This also applies to non-operating gear such as the hiking straps.

The important point to remember about the hiking straps is that if they are placed in the wrong position on the boat, you are going to be uncomfortable every time you use them. They should be so placed as to allow you maximum hiking advantage with minimum discomfort. Broad hiking straps are better than narrow ones as they spread the load on your feet. It is a great aid to wear yachting shoes when racing. Shoes will give the wearer greater comfort when tucked under a hiking strap. Ideally, the strap will be placed in such a position that when both feet are under it, your whole body is outboard of the gunwale with the lower part of your bottom just in contact with the gunwale. If the gunwale is not rounded and class rules allow it to be rounded, get to work on it. Rounding the gunwale edge will allow you to slide in and out more easily and apart from lightening your boat by a few ounces, will also add to the comfort of hiking.

how to get in and out on the trapeze. Practice on the trapeze will pay dividends and will also give a helmsman confidence.

If you sail a boat using hiking straps, you will know the importance of being quite fit so that you can continue to use your weight right throughout the race to trim your boat. It is important to remember that today's modern racing catamarans are built very light, and the position of your body on the boat will greatly affect the boat's performance. Crew weight too far forward when reaching hard may cause a capsize after nosing in. Weight too far aft when beating might not allow full upwind speed and/or a good pointing angle. It is important to stress here that

WHEN YOU ARE ALL ALONE

Assorted gear, gadgets and go-fasts are useless on a single-hander unless they can all be simply operated by the helmsman. All the important systems must be handy to the skipper's normal racing position on the boat. This Quickcat is a typical example of a well set up but simple mono-type. Sailed from a swing plank, the mainsheet and tiller extension are easy to control. Have a close look at the main hawse. It is simply a length of stainless steel rod, 1/4" in diameter, bent in a pre-determined curve. A small block on the rod carries the mainsheet block. No control rope is used or is necessary as the block always finds its own position.

If you use a hiking plank, it might pay to place foot loops on the gunwale on each side of the plank, especially if you sail in an area where the seas are lumpy. The steadying effect of foot loops can be a great advantage.

On a boat with a trapeze, foot loops are also useful if placed aft on the gunwale so that they can be used when reaching. The problem when reaching in strong winds is that as you drive the boat hard, you force the lee bow down. When enough water piles up onto the lee deck, the boat will start to trip over itself with its own forward momentum. The skipper, like the boat, has no personal brakes to apply and can be swung forward on the trapeze. The more severe the nosedive, the more suddenly the boat will stop and the harder the skipper is thrown forward. Foot loops can at least help to keep him where he wants to be. As the boat recovers, the nose lifts, the sail is hauled in again to regain power and away it goes.

Apart from wearing yachting shoes,

the single-handed cat skipper should always wear a life jacket, or at least an aid to buoyancy. He then has some protection if he should be knocked overboard or even knocked out. Today, most race committees insist on a life jacket being worn when racing. A mono-type sailor should wear one all the time when sailing. In warmer climates, shorts are commonly worn when sailing but if you have to use hiking straps, it will pay to wear a pair of special sailing trousers for any big regatta. If you find yourself in a series of races in heavy winds, you may discover that wearing trousers which are padded around the thighs will help your comfort.

In colder climates, or when racing on days when it could turn cold, you should always wear one more woollen sweater than you think you will need. These items may seem unimportant but if you get into a race and then start to feel uncomfortable, the effect over a period of time will upset your concentration and cost you the race.

On the other hand, if your mind is free from all these little things and able to concentrate on what it should be doing (that is winning the race) you will sail a much better race. Personal comfort on a single-hander is most important.

SIMPLE GADGETS

The items which require adjustment on today's modern single-handed catamarans are:
1. UNA or CAT RIG
    mast rotation device
    mainsheet traveller hawse
    mainsheet
    tack downhaul
    clew outhaul
    leech line
    centreboard uphaul-downhaul
    adjustable trapeze.

2. SLOOP RIG
    All the above items plus:
    jib barber hauler (inboard-outboard, fore and aft adjustment)
    jib luff tension.
    Additional items may be:
    diamond tension
    boom vang.

The items favoured for adjustment by the skipper from both sides of the single-handed catamaran are:
    Mast rotation.
    Mainsheet traveller hawse.
    Mainsheet.
    Centreboard uphaul-downhaul.
    and adjustable trapeze.

On a sloop, the jib luff tensioner and jib barber-hauler should both be able to be operated from either side of the cat.

The mast rotation system favoured on the International Australis was originally similar to the type first seen on the International Tornado. This system had a single rope attached to a mast rotation lever and fixed at a point aft of the lever on the underside of the boom. Variation of the length of the rope simply limited the amount of rotation.

Recently, the Australis has seen a change in this system. The disadvantage with the old method was that the skipper had to come inboard to the mast to alter mast rotation. The new system was developed at the same time as the introduction of the straight rather than curved mainbeam originally seen on the early Australis. The rotation lever is set low on the mast just above the mast step and is at ninety degrees to the centreline of the boat. A single rope leads from it through a deadeye set in the mainbeam to one side of the mast. This rope is spliced into one long rope which leads out of the beam on each side of the boat and into clam cleats or similar retaining devices. Thus the mast rotation is easily altered by the skipper, even while on the trapeze.

WHEN YOU ARE ALL ALONE   43

Some class rules do not permit a trapeze or a hiking plank so the swing strap must be used with the utmost efficiency. The strap on this Paper Tiger is too long. Although the helmsman looks comfortable enough with the boat heeled, he would have his backside in the water when the boat was level, and he would find it impossible to come aboard without using one arm which would mean momentarily releasing either the tiller or the mainsheet.

The mainsheet traveller hawse systems vary according to the preference of each skipper. The straight track-traveller with roller trolley fixed onto the aft beam is in common use today. A number of top boats, however, still favour a wire hawse with running traveller on sheaves or blocks. From the traveller is set the mainsheet block system. Adjustment of the traveller position is usually by a rope on each side of the boat running to clam cleats, cam cleats or similar fittings. An endless rope running along the aft beam and set up with considerable tension is one system sometimes used. Positioning of the traveller is easily achieved by holding the tensioned rope and either pulling it towards oneself or pushing away. No loose ropes are left lying around to catch on fittings or in blocks. The main disadvantage with this system is that adjustment is required after each tack. To adjust it whilst on the trapeze is almost impossible and therefore an adaptation has to be devised. Traveller positioning hawse systems have to be simple, workable and secure.

Mainsheet systems also vary according to individual tastes and depend on the requirements of the rig. Some skippers

Obviously not his first time in the water! This is a perfect example of how an Australis or A-class should be righted. In this position the boat will very quickly drift around so that the mast faces into the breeze. The wind on the trampoline will right the boat. As the boat comes up the crew should hang on the dolphin striker in the water to prevent a 180° flip.

may want more leech tension and therefore add a couple more purchases. Another skipper who requires less tension will have fewer blocks in the system. Mainsheet systems on any cat must run freely. In light winds, light-weight ropes were sometimes favoured but today are rarely used. The easy positioning of the sail through the traveller system and the ability easily to reduce the amount of purchase by taking the mainsheet out of a couple of blocks, has seen the adoption of one permanent mainsheet for all wind strengths.

Use of a power or ratchet block on the take-off point of the mainsheet is common. Some systems use the power or ratchet block on the boom as the last block before running the sheet through a normal block. This ensures that the complete benefit is gained by the rope's angle entering and leaving the block.

Perhaps the most important development on catamarans in recent times is a system which allows the skipper to raise his centreboards from the weather hull. The benefits of being able to do this in heavy weather are considerable. If you sail a catamaran with a system which requires you to go to leeward to raise a board you will know the frightening consequences, quite apart from not being able to concentrate on sailing your boat at its fastest speed. Here we describe the system for dagger boards:

A hole is drilled in each board, just above the keel line when the board is fully down. These holes should be large enough to take a light rope. A small piece of plastic tube can be inserted to protect the board and aid the free running of the rope. The board is then grooved on either side from the hole up to the top of the board. A small deadeye is fastened to the

WHEN YOU ARE ALL ALONE

Whether using a hiking plank or trapeze, concentration is of paramount importance.

deck either side of the platecase in line with the hole in the centreboard.

The control rope leads from the outer deadeye, down the groove in the board, through the hole and up the other side. The rope then leads through the inner deadeye and across the boat to a clam cleat or cam cleat.

This system is designed to raise the board only. It cannot be used to lower the board.

There seems to be no way of lowering the dagger board by remote control unless it is set up with strong shock cord and raised under tension. When the rope holding the board up is released, the board would be lowered by the pressure of the shock cord. With this system on an Australis, either board or both can quickly be raised and kept at the desired position until they need to be lowered.

The Tornado system, developed for pivoting centreboards, is set up with a shock cord so that the board is held up in the case by the cord. A rope is used to lower and lock the board down. The Australian Quickcat, a single-hander with a single centreboard, uses a similar system.

On a single-hander with two pivoting centreboards, shock cord is still used to raise the board. A rope is attached to the

Problems! Here Chris Wilson (150) loses half a rudder blade in a championship heat and throws up quite a rooster tail. 164 is about to scream past amid clouds of spray.

top of the board to lower it. This rope then continues through a small block set on the deck directly aft of the centreboard case, and leads at right angles through a cam cleat and across the boat to the other hull. It can be pulled by the skipper when positioned on the windward side to lower the opposite hull's centreboard. To lower the board on the windward hull when sitting on that hull, he only needs to pull the board down and lock the rope in the cleat.

The adjustable trapeze used on single-handers is similar to that used on many two-man catamarans. The end of the trapeze wire is attached to a double block, the type with a Vee slot in it to lock the rope at the desired position. The rope is led down to another double block and on the bottom of this block is set the trapeze ring. When the crew is on the trapeze he is able to adjust his height by using the block and tackle on the trapeze. There is one new addition to this system which has improved it further. A small shock cord, about four feet long, is fixed to the trapeze wire about six feet above the handle. The rope fall from the trapeze adjuster is attached to the end of the shock cord and this keeps the rope under tension and safely cleated while sailing.

Another gadget developed in conjunction with the trapeze came about because in heavy weather, the crew on trapeze can be thrown forward when reaching. On most single-handers, the mainsheet helps keep the crew in position but as he moves aft this effect is reduced. So to keep the trapeze man in place, a restraining system has been developed that prevents him swinging forward. A rope, knotted every two or three feet, is fixed to the gunwale at the transom. It leads forward to the chainplate where it runs

WHEN YOU ARE ALL ALONE

When the racing is close, you must be ready to respond immediately to a change in wind conditions. Note that Max (white shirt) has his right foot on the gunwale ready to push himself out on the plank if a puff hits. When he does this he must allow the tiller extension to slip through his hand, otherwise the boat will bear away hitting the boat to leeward.

through a small pulley, then halfway back to the stern it is attached to a shock cord. The shock cord leads back to the aft beam where it is led across to the other side of the catamaran and the system repeated. When trapezing aft, the knotted part of the rope is simply picked up and a knot placed in a hook welded onto the trapeze harness plate. The hook is made so that it just takes the knot with a limited amount of movement. The steadying effect of the extra rope on the trapeze hand is quite incredible. This system might not be used more than a few times each season when sailing in sheltered waters. But in heavy winds and bad seas, it offers exceptional security, especially in a nosedive quick-stop situation.

On sloop-rigged one-man cats, it will be an advantage to use a jib luff tensioner that can be adjusted from either side of the boat. It is equally important to set up your jib sheeting system so that the sheeting position can be adjusted forward or aft, or moved inboard or outboard as the conditions dictate. This system should be on every sloop-rigged catamaran.

Those systems which are not usually adjustable from either side are probably the most important on the boat. They mainly control the rig and sail shape. It is most important that they also are simple in design and in operation.

The tack or luff downhaul is one system that is sometimes operated on every leg of the course. Upwind, the luff is tensioned the desired amount to set the mainsail. Downwind, it is freed to move the flow of the sail aft and gain more power. On a reach it may be freed just a

In a variable breeze the bent legs position on the trapeze may prevent the boat from heeling to weather. In these conditions it is preferable to shorten the trapeze system, so that the crew can swing aboard without needing to use his hands to lift himself over the gunwale.

WHEN YOU ARE ALL ALONE

Graham Johnston, designer of the Australis, sails his boat beautifully on Sydney Harbour. Angle of heel is absolutely perfect for upwind sailing.

little. This may sound like a lot of unnecessary adjustment but the top boats are continually operating their luff tensioner.

There are many different systems in use and these have been designed to suit the needs of the particular class. The best system is the simplest system that works. So study the top boats in your class. If your class is not using a tensioner device, then look at other classes which do use them and try fitting one on your own boat.

An adjustable clew outhaul has been tried on some older single-handed cats but often ended up on the scrap heap. But now the faster modern classes are using them most of the time. The system is usually a small section of track mounted near the end of the boom with a sliding or roller traveller on it. The clew is fastened to the traveller.

The best system seen is one which was adjusted by the mainsheet tension. It was a vertically mounted lever, set into the end of the boom. From the top of the lever, a small wire was shackled to the clew of the sail. The lower part of the lever had a single pulley attached to it and this carried part of the mainsheet. As the mainsheet was hauled in for upwind work, the tension on the mainsheet increased, pulling the bottom of the lever forward and the top of the lever aft. The clew attached to the top of the lever moved aft too. Downwind, as the sheet was freed, the lever was allowed to move forward at the top (under shock cord tension) thus releasing pressure on the foot of the sail giving it more 'drive' and fullness. This system works well on any loose-footed mainsail and is ideally suited to single-handers.

Adjustable leech lines tend to be 'fashionable'. They come in and go out of favour yet most of the experts in high performing rigs do use them. If you have an adjustable leech line, ensure that it is free-running through your battens and set up to give tension where it is needed.

This Unicorn is being driven hard but as the seas appear to be reasonably smooth, the boat would sail even harder with crew weight further forward.

An adjustable leech line will allow you to carry slightly heavier battens which, under tension, can be made to give a full shape. This means a flatter sail for stronger winds. In light winds the leech line can be tensioned slightly when beating to windward to increase fullness and improve speed. It should be attached to the headboard of the sail, and it is best to set up the leech line tensioning system on the boom so that it pulls the leech wire forward and induces extra flow in the foot of the mainsail.

If, under class rules, you are permitted to adjust diamond tension when racing, it will pay to have a system to do just that. Some mono-hull classes, such as Flying Dutchman and Contender, adjust their diamond tension whilst racing but these classes do not have a rotating mast. It is common today to set up diamonds with a fair amount of slackness, and to rotate the mast about forty to forty-five degrees upwind and about ninety degrees downwind.

If, in strong winds, the sail develops too much power and the boat lifts its weather hull continually and tends to stall, you should let out your mainsheet traveller to leeward, keeping the mainsheet on fairly hard. If you still have trouble holding the boat down and driving hard, it will pay to free some sheet to relax the leech. Alternatively, it might be better to de-rotate the mast a bit so that it flattens the rig. In extreme conditions this will also safeguard your mast from breaking or over-bending.

Sailing a single-hander in a race requires a special technique. It is important to realize that your weight on a one-man catamaran is considerable when compared with the all-up weight of the boat. Consequently, you must be sure to place your weight to best advantage on the boat. In light winds, you will find

WHEN YOU ARE ALL ALONE

that you may have to sit near the mainbeam amidships to allow the boat to heel a little to leeward, immersing the leeward hull but not lifting the windward hull clear of the water. This will tend to reduce hull drag and allow the sail to 'fall' into shape and set better. The boat is more responsive and increases forward motion. It will also point higher.

In stronger winds, say a medium breeze, you will need to use the trapeze or hiking device. But if the wind is not strong enough to require all your weight on the trapeze or hiking plank, you should get into a position that will allow you to trim the craft yet still allow you to use more of your weight in a puff. On a plank, you can crouch on the gunwale and push out in a gust. On a trapeze, you can be hooked up ready to slide outboard. On a cat with only hiking straps, you can have your feet under the straps ready to hang over the gunwale.

The Hobie Cat, because of its simplicity, can be fabulous fun for the inexperienced single-handed sailor. This class also enjoys very keen one-design championship racing.

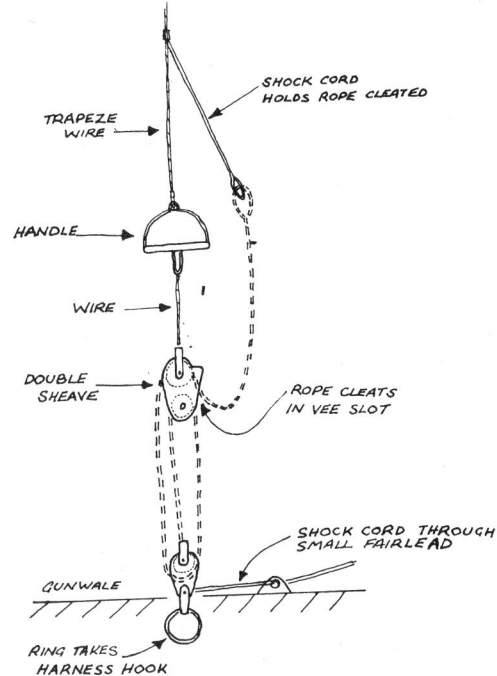

The now universally accepted trapeze adjustment method. The double sheave block with Vee cleating slot is readily available from most ship's chandlers. This system easily allows the crew to raise and lower himself whilst still flat out on the trapeze.

Rough surface adhesive tape is readily available to provide a non-slip grip for the trapeze hand's feet. This trapeze system does not include the facility to adjust the length, but it does have a two-position ring. The shock cord lifting the ring will keep the gear securely hooked to the harness when sitting on the deck between puffs.

Upwind, your weight should be placed about halfway along the hull around the centreboard position or just aft of it. In stronger winds, you may need to move aft slightly to raise the bows.

When you are shy reaching in strong winds you will need to position yourself well aft. In very light winds, however, it will be better to keep your weight forward and raise the sterns, keeping the bows deep in the water. Hull drag is reduced and speed is therefore increased. In moderate conditions, you should be ready to move your weight as the wind dictates. It is very important to realize that your body weight placement on the boat will greatly influence the trim of the craft.

On a broad reach, you will need to move aft, about halfway between the position for upwind sailing and reaching shy.

On a proud run, you must move your weight forward except in the strongest winds. This keeps the bows in the water and the sterns out. In very light winds, you might even sit to leeward. Moving your weight forward downwind also has the effect of raking the mast forward and this always seems to improve boat speed. A one-man cat can be made to sail faster by playing the waves downwind. Practise and learn this technique and use it.

Single-handed catamaran racing is probably the most rewarding type of single-handed sailing in the world today. The higher speeds make it more thrilling than mono-hull racing and it can be more demanding mentally and physically. It requires very special techniques and ingenious gear and gadgets. But it is the true 'man against man' racing that gives it such a unique appeal.

Two-Man Cat Teamwork 4

In a two-man catamaran, particularly for those who take their racing very seriously, a skipper, no matter how brilliant, cannot succeed without the support of a very good crew. In the 'big-time' classes such as the International C-class or the Tornado, the co-operation, co-ordination and teamwork of helmsman and crew is as vital to the boat's performance as the set of the sail or the bend in the mast. And a good crew is not always easy to find. Some, just a few, are naturals right from their first sail. They move catlike around the boat doing all that is asked with the minimum of fuss. But a good crew needs much more than natural ability and skill if he (or she, for that matter) is to be part of a championship victory.

We once overheard a yachting journalist asking a top catamaran skipper; 'What would happen if either you or your crew were unable to sail in tomorrow's race?' He replied, 'My boat would sail much better with a replacement skipper than with a replacement crew. My crew knows all the systems, rig adjustment, sail trim and so on. After all I just steer the boat!' Well, maybe this skipper was just being kind to his forward hand. But at least there is some truth in his comment. What he did not say, and what might well have been the case, was that his crew had been trained by him, the systems that he was so good at using were developed by the skipper, and that much of this crew's ability was due really to the skill of the skipper.

Almost without exception, the very good boats have very good crews. And of course these boats have good skippers too. The question that this raises is, does the good crew make the good skipper or does the reverse apply? We think it is a little of each. A skipper must always be in complete control of his boat and have the final say in everything that happens to the boat or on the boat. Therefore the skipper will play the major role in developing a perfect partnership with his crew. But for this relationship to develop fully, the crew must contribute ideas and be energetic, enthusiastic, agile, placid, and thinking all the time of ways to improve the teamwork on the boat.

The perfect crew probably does not exist, or at least has remained undiscovered. And as every skipper's idea of the perfect crew is slightly different, this makes it difficult to write a precise crew specification. On Australia's Little America's Cup C-class cat, *Quest III*, Bruce Proctor prefers a big, strong and quite heavy crew. Graham Ainslie, whose superb crew work during the 1972 match, was a key factor in Quest's superiority, is six foot one inch tall and weighs close to fourteen stone. He is young, very fit, immensely strong and has the stamina to perform at his best lap after lap in even the most severe conditions. Yet, on the other hand, World Tornado Champion Maurie Davies prefers a much lighter crew. His crew for the last few seasons, Ian Ramsay, is also young, fit and agile but he is only about five foot ten inches tall and weighs less than ten stone. Both these crew are most excellent and cannot be bettered anywhere in the world in any class of small sailing boat.

We have both raced as helmsman in two-man catamarans. And we have both sailed forward hand on two-man cats. Taking our own experience into account plus comments made from other skippers and crew and by observing some of the world's best, we have tried to establish the basic requirements for a good catamaran crew.

The first, and most important, requirement of a cat crew is enthusiasm. Not only an enthusiasm to go racing and to do well, but an enthusiasm towards the boat, the class, the club. In other words, the total scene. And this enthusiasm must be a long-term attitude and not just a race-day keenness to get out on the water and thrash the opposition. As a generalization, it can be said that young people tend to be more enthusiastic than those a little more mature. But in our experience, this enthusiasm of the young can run 'hot and cold'. Quite often we see the best part of a season spent by a skipper training a keen young crew only to find his time wasted when that same young fellow has his enthusiasm diverted by a new girl friend, a car, surfing, pop music, travel or whatever. So be warned and be a little wary of the short-term enthusiasm of the young.

Preferably, a crew should also have some sailing experience. And if this experience is as a skipper so much the better. Even if the experience is only of a very basic form it will still be very helpful. A crew must know how to sail the boat. He needs to understand the basics of what makes the boat go – quite apart from the need to take over when the skipper falls overboard! Possibly the best crews are those who have sailed their own mono-type (preferably a cat, but not essential) for a season or two. Often, the more experienced the crew is as a skipper,

the better crew he will make. However, these fellows are difficult to locate because, as we all know, the tendency is for 'once a skipper, forever a skipper'. If the crew is also an experienced skipper there are a number of things he can be doing during a race that would not normally be considered crew responsibilities. For example, in heavy weather he can lay the marks. In most cats in fresher winds the spray is flying about, usually into the skipper's face making the sighting of course marks extremely difficult. Not only should the crew look for the marks and tell the skipper where they are located, but a good crew will also be in a better position to decide when to tack to lay a mark. The crew should also keep the skipper informed about the position and the tactics being employed by other close rivals in the fleet. From his position on the trapeze, he has a much better view of the fleet to leeward, and he can also study the boats astern without causing the skipper to lose concentration.

And what the crew says to the skipper about the other boats is important too. A skipper does not want to hear that 'Joe Blow behind is pointing higher and going like a train'. But he would want to know that 'Joe Blow is using less mast rotation, seems to be able to point higher, and is steadily overhauling us'. In other words, the skipper will want to know 'why' as well as 'what' when being informed of the positions of competing boats.

A crew must be fit. Not a superhuman athlete capable of incredible gymnastic feats, but a person who takes special care of himself. An overweight crew is definitely taboo, unless this excess weight is carried around the head and shoulders, and somehow this never seems to be the case. A crew should have well-developed back, shoulder and arm muscles and should have staying power. A long distance runner would always be

TWO-MAN CAT TEAMWORK

Forty Tornados on the starting line requires the utmost concentration and teamwork to make a good start. At a crowded start the boat must be kept moving at all costs, even if this means sailing free to find clear wind.

preferable to a sprinter. Most of the good crew that we know partake in some physical exercise or training apart from their sailing. We suggest to any crew (or skipper, for that matter) that jogging is as good an exercise as any. If a crew jogs about two miles a day for, say, four days a week, he will be approaching a satisfactory state of fitness. Add to this about twenty push-ups a day to develop the arms and shoulders and he'll start to feel pretty good.

Stamina is far more important than strength. If strength is lacking in a crew it is relatively simple to add another purchase in the sheet or give him a greater mechanical advantage on the gear. But if he lacks stamina, it will cause problems. That jib sheet that you think is being held firm and steady may in fact be gradually eased. If you are the sort of skipper who has a frequent glance at the jib luff, and most of us are, this can have a distastrous effect on your pointing ability.

If we had our choice, what size crew should we be looking for? This is a difficult question to answer because there are many examples of boats with pre-sumably the 'wrong' size crew doing very well. There was a time when we could reliably have said that a tall heavy crew was essential for a boat to perform well in winds over twenty knots, and that two lightweights on a boat always resulted in a downwind 'flyer'. Not so today. In most classes racing today, the rig refinements are such that they allow mast bend and sail shape to be tuned to a great variety of wind and sea conditions. Likewise, the rig can and should be set up to suit the particular crew weight of the boat. But if we were forced into a corner and had to nominate the size of our perfect crew, he would be something like this: Tall, say around six foot, with long powerful legs and narrow hips. He would have very little tummy, broad shoulders, and strong arms and shoulders. He should weigh from ten and a half to eleven and a half stone.

And finally our crew should have the right mental attitude. No doubt that can be said about any top sportsman, but in a two-man sailing boat great demands are placed on the character of both skipper and crew. A crew must be absolutely

With good crew work, a Tornado can be driven very hard to windward in fresh winds. Here Ditto 4's *crew, Robin Rust, is low on the trapeze wire with legs straight, one hand holds the jib sheet, the other is raised for added leverage. Note that he wears sailing shoes.*

reliable. Of course, he must arrive for sailing on or before the time he is expected, and not leave until the boat is completely unrigged and all work finished. But he must be reliable, or perhaps dependable is a more apt word, during a race. A skipper must know exactly what his crew will do in any given situation. If the lee bow starts to bury, he wants to know that the crew is already moving aft behind him, without being asked. And he wants to know that the crew will do this *every* time.

A two-man racing catamaran brings two people, skipper and crew, together sometimes for quite long periods. It takes great strength of character for them not to have frequent disagreements. During a race a skipper is often under very great mental pressure, particularly while starting or in a tacking duel approaching the finishing line. A crew must understand this and offer encouragement and never criticism. In fact, a good crew will *never* criticize his skipper, either to his face or behind his back. If the skipper has any talent at all he will know when he has made mistakes without being told. And naturally a good skipper will *never, never* blame his crew for his own mistakes nor criticize his crew in public.

So much for the type (and shape) of person that you should seek in a crew. Now let us look at some of the skipper/crew techniques that can be developed for better racing performance.

Rigging the boat. Most sailors probably treat the rigging and preparation of their boat before a race as a fairly routine and basic procedure. And so it is if you go about it in a methodical manner. We

TWO-MAN CAT TEAMWORK

remember our days of dinghy sailing when, as we pushed off the beach, one of us would say to the other, 'Did you put the bungs in?' And we remember how often we looked over the transom to find them still open!

The main point about skipper/crew technique in rigging and preparing the boat is to establish a set routine, with each of you performing the same tasks each time you get the boat ready for the water. Stepping the mast is a good example. One of you should *always* take the forestay and the other *always* stand on the trampoline to lift the mast. It is not a bad idea if the taller of the two is on the trampoline. If you can establish a set routine you will find that the boat will be ready much quicker and you will leave fewer things undone. How often have you stepped the mast only to find the wind indicator still in the sail bag? Or looked at the side stay adjuster plates to find one pin three holes from the top and the other side three holes from the bottom!

In establishing this set routine for rigging the boat and preparing for sailing, each of you should assume the responsibility for checking the gear. Are the shackle pins tight? Are the sail battens securely fastened? Is the trapeze rubber frayed? Are all the blocks free and running smoothly and the tracks clear of sand? Are all the sheets clear? Are they threaded the correct way through the ratchet blocks with figure-of-eight knots in the end? Are there any chips in the leading and trailing edges of the centreboards or rudder that need filling? Is there a protest flag aboard? Who has the race instructions? Have the race committee announced the course and what is it? If it is a long race, have you something to eat and drink? And so it goes on. A long list of individually basic and simple items that on their own seem unimportant but assembled together make up a well-prepared racing catamaran.

Who should be responsible for each item is largely a matter for the skipper and crew to work out together. And, of course, the overall responsibility for seeing that the boat is ready for racing must lie with the skipper because he is in charge. However, as a basic guide to better boat preparation and rigging, we have attempted to allocate the main duties to either skipper or crew, or both.

Skipper
Rudders and tillers.
Mainsail.
Mainsail battens.
Mainsheet and traveller.
Leech wire.
Mast, standing rigging.
Halyards, halyard locks.
Mast head fly.
Jib (which one).
Mast rake.
Sailing instructions.
Race entry.
Stop watch or timer.
Protest flag.

Crew
Jib battens.
Jib sheets.
Trapeze gear.
Centreboards.
Trampoline lacing.
Mast rotation gear.
Hull finish.
Food and/or drink.
Spare shackles, cord etc.
Shackle key, tools.
Both
Jib luff tension.
Mainsail luff tension.
Jib sheeting position.
Course.

Before the start. As a general rule most boats in any race leave too little time between leaving the beach and the starting time. So often you see boats arriving at a start only minutes before the Blue Peter is lowered. It is easy to underestimate the time it will take to sail out to the committee boat so make sure that you are in the vicinity of the starting line at least twenty or thirty minutes before the scheduled starting time.

When you are sailing out to the starting line you should be checking with your crew that all the gear is adjusted correctly. Check the sheeting positions, leech line, main traveller, trapeze gear and mast rotation. Then have a good look at the conditions. Watch other boats. Look at how they are sailing. Is the wind steady or gusty and is the direction steady or shifting? And most important, discuss all aspects of the conditions with your crew.

When you reach the starting line, sail over to the committee boat and say hello, or at least give a friendly wave. After all, they have given up their time so that you may race so look as though you are pleased to see them and are looking forward to the race. Some race instructions will actually require each boat to report in to the committee boat before the race. So if this is stipulated, sail near the stern of the boat (do not show off!) and call out your sail number loudly. Make sure that the Officer-of-the-day on board acknowledges your call.

Having completed the formalities, you should make two dummy starts, one on each tack, sailing through about the middle of the line. Not only will this be a check that all the gear is set up correctly for the first windward leg, but it will also give you some idea as to which end of the starting line might be favoured. Again it is most important to discuss all aspects of the start with your crew. Work out between you the sort of start that you think will put you in the best position and also discuss an alternative start if the first becomes hopeless because of the tactics of your opponents. The skipper must, of course, always make the final decision about what tack to start on, what part of the line, and on what line the approach should be made.

During the before-start manœuvring the crew has two important duties. Firstly, he must keep his eye on the rest of the fleet and warn the skipper if avoiding action might be necessary. And, secondly he must keep a very sharp watch on the

Miss Nylex *on a tight reach shows good crew readiness. It seems that wind conditions were gusty because John Buzaglo has one hand on the trapeze handle to swing aboard if not required. But he also has the crew restraining line in the other hand to prevent him swinging forward in the event of a sudden gust. In this situation the skipper can remain in the one place controlling mainsheet and helm.*

committee boat for the ten-minute signal. Watching for the ten-minute gun is made even more difficult if you have been unable to get 'starter's time' before leaving the beach. A keen-eyed crew will see the race committee readying the course flag and loading the starting gun. Most race committees throughout the world

TWO-MAN CAT TEAMWORK

Bruce Proctor with crew Graham Ainslie always seemed to sail Quest III *superbly well and* Quest III *was at her best to windward with them separated like this.*

use a shot gun with blank cartridges for the timing signals. The crew should watch the person with the gun and when he sees the gun raised in the air he should call 'gun's up', to the skipper. This will usually give the skipper enough time to be ready to set his watch or start his stop-watch when the gun is fired.

The start. The actual starting tactics are discussed elsewhere in this book so let us continue to look at the specific duties of skipper and crew during the starting operation. At this stage the ten-minute signal has just been given and we have set our watches. Whether the skipper or crew should carry the starting watch, and what type of watch this should be, is a matter of personal preference and trial and error. There are now some excellent yacht timers available but not many of these are fully waterproof. Therefore great care must be taken in sealing the watch in plastic bags and the like, because as we all know, we will get very wet sailing cats. The advantage of a proper yacht timer is that it is designed to count off backwards the time left before a start. This makes it very quick and easy to read. The major disadvantage is that it hangs on a cord around the neck and must always be held in one hand to be read.

Actually, we favour the fully waterproof wrist watch of the diver's type. This features a rotating bezel that can be moved through 360 degrees. The perfect solution is for both skipper *and* crew to wear a watch. Then the skipper can keep his own check on the number of minutes remaining but can ask the crew to call off those vital last thirty seconds when the skipper is concentrating on sailing the boat into position. It also reduces the chances of a timing error.

Whatever timing method you finally decide on, it is most important that you commence your count-down at the ten-minute signal and double-check the timer at the five-minute gun.

When the course signal is hoisted, usually at the ten-minute signal, the crew should identify the signal for the skipper; e.g. 'Red flag means the port hand course' or 'Red, white and blue vertical is numeral 3. Course three is southerly, three times around, starboard hand, finish at windward mark', and so on. Of course the skipper should also have a quick glance at the signal and confirm the course. If it is necessary to look at the course in the sailing instructions, the crew should read aloud the full details.

Max Press pushes his Tornado along very nicely in a brisk breeze. The crew is well balanced with legs slightly bent to absorb shock as the boat drops over each wave. The boat is sitting beautifully with the lee transom almost clear of the water. The crew is not wearing sailing shoes and should be; one stubbed toe in a crisis can lose the race.

On a two-man boat the crew must share the responsibility for sailing the boat and choosing the best course. Graham Ainslie here indicates to his skipper that they should gybe soon to head for the leeward mark.

TWO-MAN CAT TEAMWORK

Having already decided your preferred starting tactics, you should be in position to approach the start very soon after the five-minute signal. Whoever is keeping the time should call out aloud the time remaining every thirty seconds, thus 'four and a half', 'four minutes' and so on. With one minute to go, the time should be called off every ten seconds, 'fifty', 'forty' and so on. The final ten seconds should be called by the crew. While manœuvring for the start, taking care to watch the time and look out for other boats and wind shifts, the crew must also be ready to act immediately on the skipper's instructions. It might be necessary to tack very quickly and he must be ready. Or it might be a matter of backing the jib to slow the boat down or prevent her from going into irons. In a very tight start it might even be necessary to fend off another boat!

Immediately after the start, both skipper and crew must attempt to put right out of their minds all the drama that might have just taken place in making a start. There should be one thought and one thought only in their minds, particularly if sailing in clear wind. That is to get the boat sailing at her best and settled down as quickly as possible. This is not the time to worry about sheeting positions, mast rotation, luff tension or any of the other little things that might require adjustment as the race progresses. Do not try and point too high at this stage. Just keep the boat sailing as steadily and as fast as you can to clear yourself from the 'ruck'. Once you have the boat sailing well and are on your way to the windward mark, your crew should give you a brief run-down on the relative positions of the other boats in the fleet, particularly those boats that are difficult to see from the helmsman's position and those that you consider to be your main rivals. The crew should pay particular attention to any boats that might have tacked away from the main fleet and try and evaluate their performance. Do they appear to have more or less wind? Do they appear to be gaining tidal advantage? Are they locals

This is an Australian Stingray class cat, 18' long with an 8' beam and only slightly less sail area than a Tornado. These boats are capable of developing tremendous power, hence the need for both skipper and crew to use the trapeze. In this class good teamwork can really pay dividends.

or visitors (very important in tricky waters)? Having looked at the rest of the fleet the skipper and crew should quickly assess the performance of their own boat. Should anything be altered? Sheeting positions? Luff tensions? Mast rotation? Foot outhaul? And if you decide that some small adjustment is needed, should it be done immediately, during the next tack or can it wait until the next work to windward?

Tacking. Tacking a two-man catamaran is very much a matter of teamwork. Most two-man cats carry headsails, therefore they tack relatively easily. However, it cannot be disputed that a cat is often fairly slow through the wind, and an improvement in tacking technique can mean valuable seconds or even minutes gained around a racing course. Once again, it is a matter of developing teamwork or a set routine that is followed through *every* tack.

No doubt each class, because it differs from another, will require its own special techniques when tacking. But the similarities of the various classes are far greater than the differences. So the basic tacking procedure employed on the International Tornado should be applicable to most of the popular two-man cats around the world.

The first important point is for both the skipper and crew to know exactly when the tack is to take place. This may sound very basic yet how many skippers have been guilty of tacking without properly warning his crew only to leave them dangling on the trapeze, stranded to leeward? We think most have committed this sin at one time or another.

And the decision to tack might not always be that of the skipper. Often the crew is in a better position to sight a mark, or another boat approaching on starboard tack. If this is the case the crew

Another view of the Stingray shows the great teamwork between helmsman and forward hand. When the breeze lightens the crew is the first to move in off the trapeze, leaving the skipper steady on the wire to control the boat.

should say to his skipper, 'I think we should tack in about fifty yards'. The skipper then can still give the command to tack, as he always should do.

There are many different ways of telling a crew that you are about to tack but we have yet to find anything better than the rather old and traditional, 'Ready about', 'Yes', 'Lee'ho'.

The skipper calls, 'Ready about?' As soon as he is ready, the crew answers, 'Yes' or 'OK'. And the skipper calls 'Lee'ho' as he puts down the helm. Sounds a little corny and archaic but it certainly works!

Of course the actual words can be different but the basic format of firstly the

TWO-MAN CAT TEAMWORK

Quite apart from the clear view of Quest III's *split level bridgedeck and the tubular fore and aft bracing of the radial hawse, this picture does show the comfortable positions of both skipper and crew for upwind sailing.*

question of 'Are you ready to tack?', then the reply of 'Yes, go ahead', and finally the call of 'Well, here goes!' seems to be essential for a smooth well-executed tack.

So now let us look at a typical tack in a boat of the Tornado type and examine, step by step, the tasks of both skipper and crew. Let us assume that the wind is about fifteen knots and that the seas are no rougher than moderate.

Immediately the skipper calls, 'Ready about?' the crew will have three main things to attend to. Firstly, the jib sheet must be uncleated, but without changing the tension on the jib sheet itself. (Many skippers will not allow their crew to cleat the jib so this may not apply.) Secondly, the crew should look down to leeward just to make sure that the gear on the trampoline has not become hopelessly tangled, or that there are no other problems requiring attention before the tack. And, thirdly, he should grab the trapeze handle, ready to swing aboard. Meanwhile, the skipper should quickly check that his mainsheet and traveller gear is all set for the new tack. As soon as the crew is ready, in say five seconds he should say 'OK' or 'Ready' or a similar reply. It is quite important, however, that he always gives the same reply so that the skipper will know immediately that he can tack.

The skipper will then choose what he feels is the best wave condition and boat attitude for a smooth tack, and call 'Lee'ho'. At this stage the crew is still out on the trapeze. The moment the skipper calls, he should put the helm down. Not too suddenly or the boat will stop, but as the boat approaches head-to-wind, the amount of helm can be increased. As soon as the mainsail loses wind the mainsheet should be eased and about five or six feet of rope released. The skipper should then move very quickly to the other side of the boat, keeping the helm over the whole time. Before the main fills on the new tack he should check that the traveller is in the correct position, make sure that he has at least one foot under the swing strap, and be ready to harden the sheet as the boat gets moving on the new tack.

Meanwhile the crew has been very busy! On the skipper's call of 'Lee'ho', the crew should swing in off the trapeze and unhook as quickly as possible. He should also ease the jib sheet slightly but definitely not let it go altogether as a flogging headsail will stop the boat dead in no time at all. The crew keeps control of the jib sheet throughout the tack and at this stage he is still probably on the weather side of the boat as the jib starts to back. At this point he should duck under the boom picking up the new jib sheet with his free hand. As soon as the boat is through head-to-wind he should completely release the jib which by now is aback, and steadily haul in the new sheet. The jib sheet should never be jerked in hard, but should be steadily hardened as the speed of the boat increases. The crew should have the jib sheet in one hand, the hand opposite to where the trapeze wire is located. With his other hand he takes the trapeze wire and hooks on. As the boat picks up speed and develops heel, the skipper will be hardening the mainsheet and the crew should be out on the trapeze if conditions require this. The boat will now be close to top speed on the opposite tack and the crew should make the final adjustment of the jib sheet tension. The jib sheet may then be cleated.

Many skippers think that the cleating of the jib sheet is a very bad idea and do not provide their crew with cam or clam cleats for this purpose. We feel that in steady wind conditions a cleated jib has an important advantage over a sheet held in the hand all the time. No matter how hard a crew might try and how strong and dedicated he might be, it is almost impossible to maintain a constant setting on the jib sheet, particularly in fresher winds. If the skipper is to sail the boat at her best upwind it is imperative that he find the optimum jib sheet setting and that it remains constant for the entire leg. Modern-day cam cleats and clam cleats are very efficient and most effective if well located for the crew. The cleats must be located in such a way that they allow the crew to make sheet adjustments while stretched out on the trapeze.

In variable sailing conditions it is an entirely different matter. When the wind is continually gusting and easing it is most important for the crew to retain complete control of the jib and not cleat the sheet. The jib will need to be hardened in the gusts and eased again when they have passed.

Rounding marks. We have now made a good start, got the boat moving well upwind, put in some superb tacks and are approaching the weather mark. Let us assume that we are to round the mark to starboard and that we have just tacked onto a port tack to lay the mark. Again using the Tornado as an example (but most sloop-rigged two-man cats would have very similar gear), we have listed most of the tasks that either the skipper or crew would perform immediately after rounding the windward mark to the return leg of a 'windward and return' course. The letters 's' or 'c' indicate which member of the team, skipper or crew, would perform the tasks. This could vary

TWO-MAN CAT TEAMWORK

Both skipper and crew work to drive this Manta hard. The crew has his trapeze wire long for greatest advantage. The skipper could do with a more neatly fitting spray jacket to reduce windage.

considerably depending on the particular class, the way the equipment is set up and the preferences of the crew in developing teamwork.

  Ease jib sheet. (c)
  Re-set jib sheet traveller to leeward. (s)
  Raise leeward centreboard. (c)
  Half raise weather centreboard. (s)
  Fully rotate mast. (c)
  Ease jib luff down-haul. (c)
  Ease mainsheet. (s)
  Re-set main traveller to leeward. (s)
  Tighten leech line. (s)
  Adjust mainsail foot batten control to increase fullness. (c)
  Move weight forward to keep transoms out of water. (s and c)

And to this list must be added other less specific items such as looking for the next mark, watching your main opponents, looking for special wind or tidal advantages and, above all, keeping the boat moving at top speed all the time.

There is no substitute for practice when it comes to rounding marks in a highly competitive situation. If you can get all your gear adjusted with the minimum of jumping around the boat and the minimum of time, and have your boat sailing fast on the new leg of the course very soon after rounding the mark, it can make that little difference between winning a race and narrowly losing. Here again, it is worth watching closely the better boats in your racing fleet. These good boats always seem to bolt away soon after rounding a mark yet for the remainder of that particular leg they may not increase their lead a great deal more. Why is this so?

The main reason for this common occurrence is that on these better boats the skipper and crew are a team and they have practised together long enough to know exactly what to do after rounding the mark. They know the precise setting for every piece of gear. They also know exactly what jobs are theirs to perform

C

Robin Rust rides the wire on Chris Wilson's Australian Champ, Yvonne 20. The boat here is obviously over-powered and they are riding out a puff. But have a closer look at this picture and you will see that tucked away behind the main and jib is 175 square feet of spinnaker.

and go about them coolly and swiftly. Consequently, they are able to get the boat around the mark and sailing at her best on the new leg of the course while others in the fleet are still fiddling about with their gear trying to find the correct setting.

Gybing. Unlike gybing some of the popular but very tender dinghies, gybing a catamaran is a relatively basic and straightforward operation. Like tacking, it is most important for the skipper to give the crew some warning before making the gybe. The crew should check that the gear is ready for the other tack and the skipper should check that the main traveller is free to move right across the boat to the new leeward side. If the crew has been perched on the leeward bow for the downwind leg, he will need to move aft onto the trampoline during the gybe itself.

Only in very heavy conditions will it be necessary for the skipper to haul in the mainsheet before allowing the boom to swing across. In most conditions it is quite all right to let the boom 'crash' across from one side to the other. If there is any sea running at all, the gybe will always be quicker, smoother and more graceful if completed while riding a wave. In moderate seas it is possible to sail down the face of a wave, complete the gybe, and get sailing on the new tack, all while still riding the one wave. Try to perfect this if you do much sailing in open waters.

TWO-MAN CAT TEAMWORK

Reaching. The beam reach can be the most demanding point of sailing for a cat skipper and crew. It can also be incredibly fast and exciting. Also, the courses that are being set for cats today make it absolutely critical that you are able to sail your boat fast on a beam reach.

Things can become somewhat dramatic when on a tight reach in a moderate to fresh breeze. On rounding the mark it will be necessary to make some adjustment to the rig but to a lesser degree than for the freer legs. If the wind is over about fifteen knots it will be necessary to raise the leeward centreboard to prevent the boat 'tripping', and the main traveller should also be eased one or two feet off centre.

The trick in sailing a cat well on a reach in fresh conditions is in keeping the weight sufficiently far forward to prevent the transoms from dragging, yet far enough aft to prevent the lee bow from burying. This cannot be done effectively without some very nimble footwork on the part of the crew. The crew on the trapeze should move up and down along the gunwale from as far forward as the mast to as far aft as standing with one foot either side of the skipper. As the crew moves aft, away from the mast, the trapeze wire will have the apparent effect of shortening, causing the crew to be more upright. This can have a disastrous effect if a sudden gust causes the weather hull to fly very high. Because the crew is standing more upright, and because in his position aft near the skipper he is not as well balanced, he is likely to topple over the skipper's head to land with a terrible crash on the trampoline down to leeward.

To overcome this, an adjustable-length trapeze wire is now commonly used. This is simply a small three-to-one purchase between the trapeze handle and the ring that enables the crew to raise and lower himself while still on the trapeze. Most of these work very well but the system does

The Cunningham designed B-class Mehitabel, *sailed by Peter Blaxland, finished second to the Tornado in the IYRU selection trials. The wind is very fresh here and Peter is sailing a little easily as he heads for the leeward mark on Sydney Harbour. Skipper/crew teamwork is of paramount importance in cat racing and no skipper can perform at his best without a good, well-trained crew.*

require a high degree of skill to get the most out of it. For not only does the crew lengthen the trapeze wire as he moves aft, thus maintaining a constant angle to the boat, but he must also raise himself on the wire as he moves forward. And he must do all this while keeping complete control over the jib sheet. So our advice is to fit an adjustable-length

Concentration is the key to success in most sailing conditions but especially when the wind is gusty. Here the crew has his trapeze wire long for maximum power in the gusts but has his knees bent when the boat levels.

trapeze system but to practise and practise with it before placing too much faith in it for major events.

Conclusion. Sailing a two-man racing boat, especially a catamaran, is unquestionably a team effort. It is the co-ordination and co-operation between skipper and crew that brings about success in two-man racing and it is the development of this teamwork that can be so rewarding. We believe that there are a great number of cat skippers sailing today, many of them in mono-types, who would find their sailing much more rewarding if they joined forces with someone and took up a two-man class. Some might be reluctant to give up being a skipper and take on crewing. But the important thing about racing is to do well and to make the very best use of your experience and own particular ability.

A mediocre skipper may well make a first class crew, and as such can perhaps enjoy greater racing successes than he could ever have achieved on his own.

And, finally, a word about the not-so-good crew. If you find that your crew is inclined to be unreliable, lacking in enthusiasm, not a good mover around the boat, but a great guy all the same — do not persevere with him. A good crew can make a good skipper but a bad one rarely will. And anyhow, why should you let anyone else spoil your racing? Life is too short for that.

'Drifter' Racing Can Be Fun 5

Catamarans have become popular throughout the world because of their reputation for being very fast in a good breeze. But unfortunately some of the early cat designs did not perform well at all in light airs. And cat sailors in those days had not yet developed the special techniques necessary to keep a boat moving when the wind is scarce. The cat designs of today such as the Australis and the Tornado with their taller rigs and more sophisticated sail control, have changed this. Also catamaran yachtsmen today are more skilful. Their improved skill has helped in bringing about a change of attitude whereby cats can now be considered all-weather craft.

We all know that cat racing is usually more fun in a fresh breeze. However, with the right mental approach and sailing technique, light weather racing can be equally rewarding. Many of us only enjoy our racing if the wind is over, say, ten knots. If it is less than this we might be inclined to lose interest. Or even convince ourselves that the race is likely to be won on luck rather than ability, so what is the point in trying?

LUCK OR SKILL?

After a light weather race, how often do we hear comments like, 'He only won because of a twenty-degree wind shift on the final work!' or 'He carried a private breeze for the whole of the downwind leg!' and so on. These excuses are used primarily by skippers who have the basic ability to perform well but have not quite found the secret to light weather racing.

Certainly luck does play a part in light weather racing, sometimes resulting in the most incredible frustration. But watch the good boats in the fleet. Somehow the good skippers usually seem to have their boats in the best position to take advantage of the slightest catspaw or wind shift. The good boats never seem to stop moving at any stage, while others in the fleet drift hopelessly without wind at all. And that is certainly not all luck. Keeping the boat moving, being in the right position, being able to make the best use of the breeze when your turn comes, are all factors in light weather technique.

BASIC DIFFERENCES

Those of us who have been fortunate enough to race mono-hull boats find that there are not so very many differences when it comes to getting the best out of a cat. However, when racing a cat in light airs, there are some characteristics that are not found in other dinghy classes. A cat is bulkier than its mono-hull counterpart, and because of this it will not handle a sloppy sea particularly well. A cat will always have a tendency to 'hobby horse' if there are seas left over from a stronger wind that has blown earlier in the day. In these conditions a cat must always be kept moving even if it means sailing a little free. Any attempt to 'pinch' when sailing to windward will result in the boat stopping dead. So dead, in fact, that you may

69

Weathercock, showing superb light weather downwind sailing technique. The boom downhaul on a radial hawse has the leech standing straight, the mast is well rotated, and the clew outhaul is adjusted to bag foot. The crew lies on forward deck of the lee hull to keep the bow in the water. The skipper also has his weight forward and is nicely placed to see the wind indicator on the leading edge of mast. This was Weathercock's *best point of sailing.*

need to drift astern on reverse rudder to get moving again. A cat is also slower to respond to the puffs in extremely light airs. It will take quite a few seconds before the boat will be moving well in the new breeze, and if this new breeze is a 'lift' great care must be taken to luff slowly or the advantage will be lost.

As we all know, a cat is slower to tack than most dinghies. If there are any seas running and the wind is fickle, tacking will be even more difficult.

SETTING UP THE BOAT

If you see that you are in for a light weather race and you are reasonably sure that it will stay that way for the whole race, there are a number of things you can do before leaving the beach to prepare yourself and the boat for the conditions. An obvious move is to put your light battens in the mainsail. But a word of caution here. In tuning your boat you should try as hard as you possibly can to have the boat perform well in all conditions using the one set of battens. If you have more than one set of battens you will find with almost monotonous frequency that you are using 'the wrong battens'. Quite apart from any effect this might have on the performance of the boat, it has a devastating effect on the confidence of the skipper and crew. If you find after much perseverance that the battens that work so well in the fresh breezes just will not do the trick, try replacing just the top two or three with lighter material.

A good, sensitive and well-balanced wind indicator is essential. The most accurate is at the mast-head. But with the top of the mast sometimes very high and difficult to see, the indicator may be best located elsewhere. Strands of light

'DRIFTER' RACING CAN BE FUN

wool on the side stays or forestays are of some help and there is now a trend towards having indicators located on pedestals on the bow or forward of the tack of the jib. Whatever form of indicator is used it must be sensitive, balanced and in undisturbed air.

Set the mainsail as high as possible on the mast keeping the luff tension firm but not really bounced down hard. If the jib has a luff tension adjuster, this should be set a little less firm than for heavier winds. But the jib luff should still be firm enough to hold a slight 'knuckle' along the luff.

For upwind sailing in light airs the mainsheet traveller should be set in the centre of the hawse. In fact, if your mainsail is cut a little flat, it might be necessary to sheet it with the traveller slightly to weather of centre. By doing this a flat sail can be sailed a little eased to induce fullness. The jib sheet position, if adjustable, should be moved aft and inboard. This enables the jib to be set close to the mainsail without being sheeted in hard. In extremely light conditions, a jib is best sheeted with the crew down on the leeward hull, holding the sheets in his hand. He will have a much more sensitive 'feel' of the sail in this position, and he will also be able to support in his hand the weight of the sheets that might otherwise hold the jib leech unnecessarily tight.

The mast and rigging will require special attention. The mast should be set up near vertical or perhaps raked slightly forward. Rarely do you see a boat with the mast raked aft perform well in light airs. If your class rules allow diamond stays and jumper stays, these should be adjusted to reduce the fore-and-aft mast bend to a minimum. This applies particularly to the few feet above the hounds. In classes like the Tornado where the allowed rigging is kept to a minimum, the diamonds should be set quite tight and the mast fully rotated through ninety degrees.

The foot batten should be slackened so that it can bend and induce flow into the lower area of the mainsail. An external leech wire will be essential for downwind racing in light breezes and it should be given a very generous tug after rounding the weather mark. In very light airs it might be worth trying a little leech line upwind just to add 'bag' to the mainsail. But be careful. Too much leech line will badly hook the leech and distort the sail shape.

STARTING

The lighter the wind, the nearer you should stay to the line immediately before the start. Light winds can be very unpredictable. They have a habit of fading in those last precious minutes or sharply shifting direction. So do not leave yourself stranded away from the line. Stay close and above all keep moving. In drifting conditions it is always more important to cross the starting line soon after the gun and moving at maximum speed than to be at the so-called 'top of the line'. In a big fleet there is usually tremendous congestion near the committee boat, with everyone vying for that coveted 'starboard tack, weather boat' position. There is often a lot of pushing and shoving and strong language, with boats barging the line and others in irons, all adding to the chaos! If you choose to join the mêlée you just might fluke a good start. On the other hand, you could very easily find that you are forced over the line early, involved in a protest, or at best, trapped in amongst a number of boats unable to tack and break into clear wind. So our advice is that unless one end of the line is very heavily favoured, keep away from the mob and try to make your own start moving fast in clear wind.

During the last few minutes before the start, watch very closely for a wind shift

Quest III *sails on a broad reach in choppy seas and light winds. Her bow mounted wind indicators and mainsail windows with ribbons were most effective in these conditions.*

and be ready to take advantage of it. The lighter the breeze the more likely this is to occur. Have a good look at the starting line and determine which end might be favoured. In most starts in large fleets you should plan to start on starboard tack unless the line is so badly laid that it will be difficult to cross on starboard. With about two minutes to go to the starting signal, try and be in a position about fifty yards to leeward of the line and about the same distance to starboard of the starboard end of the line. Have your boat on starboard tack moving very slowly with the sheets well eased. It is absolutely essential to keep the boat moving all the time and always to have steerage way.

As you start sailing for the line there will doubtless be boats ahead of you. Most of these will be trying to slow down to avoid being early, so free away and sail to leeward of them. It does not really matter if you have to sail through the lee of five or six boats as long as you keep moving all the time and are not getting so far down the line that you run a risk of not being able to lay the leeward starting mark.

With about fifteen seconds to go, harden sheets and head for the line. You should cross somewhere near the middle of the line with clear wind and sailing fast.

Sometimes, during these pre-start manœuvres it will become necessary to slow your boat down. The natural way to do this is to luff. But in a cat a sudden luff can put the boat into irons, totally out of control; a hopeless position to be caught

'DRIFTER' RACING CAN BE FUN

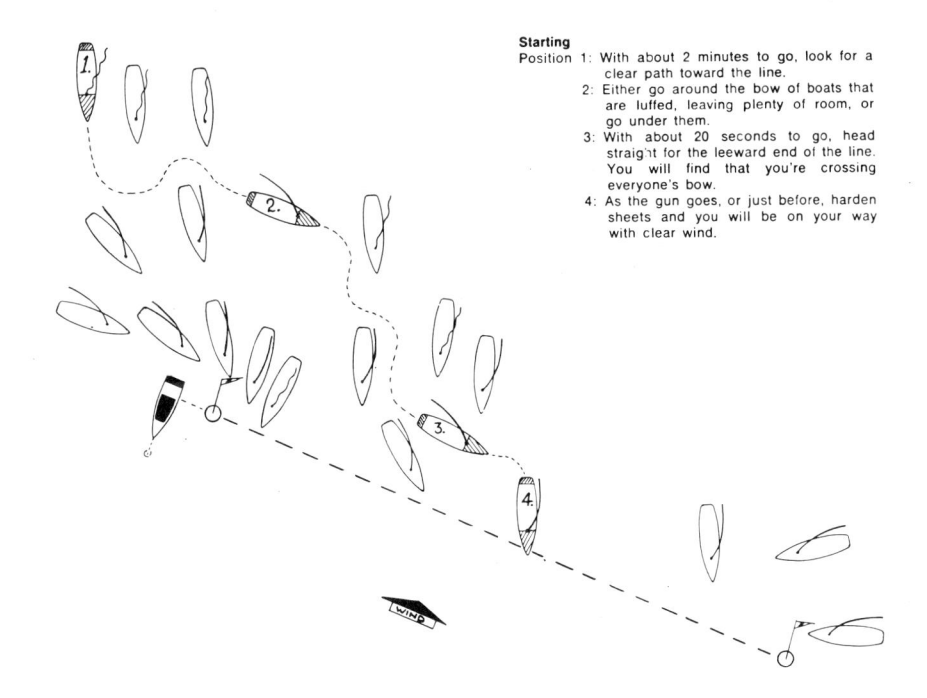

Starting
Position 1: With about 2 minutes to go, look for a clear path toward the line.
2: Either go around the bow of boats that are luffed, leaving plenty of room, or go under them.
3: With about 20 seconds to go, head straight for the leeward end of the line. You will find that you're crossing everyone's bow.
4: As the gun goes, or just before, harden sheets and you will be on your way with clear wind.

in just before the start. There is a more effective and more positive way of slowing a cat down using the rudder. Firstly, luff hard by pushing the helm right down quickly. Just as the boat starts to luff, savagely pull the helm right up. When the boat starts to bear away, repeat the first movement. A catamaran can remain almost stationary using this method yet also remain completely in control of the skipper. But remember, it does require violent movement of the helm from one side to the other, stalling out the rudders to keep the boat from accelerating.

Presuming that you have succeeded in getting a reasonably good start near the middle of the line and have clear wind, resist the temptation to tack immediately. Even if you do not have clear wind it is often better to wait a minute or two for the fleet to break up. It then gives you an opportunity to decide which side of the course you want to work, see where your main rivals are, and select the right moment to tack when you will have the least possible interference from starboard tack boats above you. If you are being covered by a boat to weather and there is clear water to leeward, try sailing a little free to break through his lee. The amount of distance lost in this is almost certain to be less than that lost in tacking.

It is also important in those few minutes after a start to sit very still on the boat and not to start fiddling with gear, making adjustments that might temporarily slow the boat.

THE WINDWARD LEG

Movement on the boat by the helmsman or the crew (if you have one) will certainly slow the boat in light airs. If you must move, do it very slowly with a minimum of jerky movement. The term 'cat-like' is often used to describe the movement of a

C*

really good light weather crew. This may sound like a very basic instruction for light weather sailing but so often this fundamental rule is ignored.

We have seen boats that are being quite well sailed to windward lose a great amount of distance just in tacking because of crew movement. In an attempt to tack quickly, the crew leaps about all over the place freeing sheets and pulling others, while the boat stops dead. If the wind is very light the crew should remain in the same position until the tack is completed with the boat sailing on the new tack. He can then carefully move into his correct position.

The actual position for both skipper and crew or the skipper alone on a mono-type, is really one of personal preference and trial and error. There are however a few 'ground rules' that should be observed. It is important to keep the boat slightly heeled to leeward. Not only does this help the sails fall into shape but it does keep the leeward hull deep in the water, making full use of the water-line length. The boat will point higher in this attitude. But this heeling to leeward should not be taken to extremes. Some skippers even have their crews trapeze to leeward to keep the boat heeled. Rarely does this result in any advantage. Most often the movement of the boat caused by the crew getting out on the wire and getting comfortable far outweighs any benefits gained from an increase in heel. In most mono-types the boat can be adequately heeled with the skipper sitting or lying amidships. In most two-man cats the crew can lie along the leeward hull. Most cats have a transom and it is important to keep this clear of the water to avoid drag. Crew weight must be positioned well forward as well as being to leeward.

Quite often light weather races are sailed in conditions that are constantly variable. This comment applies particularly to inland waters. In these conditions it is not simply a matter of placing your crew in the best position to balance the boat — both skipper and crew must be in a position fully to capitalize on the puffs when they come. If the crew is sprawled along the leeward foredeck, then the skipper will need to be able to move quickly to 'ride' the puffs. It is possible to half-sit, half-lie in the trampoline with one foot still under the swing strap so that when the puff hits (and you should see it coming across the water), you simply sit on the deck and swing out as required. If the puff is harder than expected but does not look as though it will last for very long, it is better to ease the sheet a little and hold the boat flat in your present positions rather than the crew scrambling across the trampoline from his position to leeward to sit on the weather hull.

Regardless of the strength of the wind, no cat can ever hope to sail well to windward unless it has clear air. And this is even more critical in light winds. If you are being covered by another boat you will need to tack to break clear. But as every tack you make will lose you distance they should be kept to a minimum. You should try and choose a course to sail that will make it difficult for your opponents to work into a covering position. This does not mean that you should take a 'flyer' and go off on your own, but it is possible to keep on the opposite tack to your main rivals. You should at least try to approach the weather mark on the opposite tack. And remember that if you are to round the weather mark to starboard, it could be well worth while to approach the mark on port tack rather than the more conventional starboard tack. If there are a few boats approaching the mark on starboard tack and they are likely to claim you on 'starboard', slightly over lay the mark but still approach it on

'DRIFTER' RACING CAN BE FUN

port tack. Even if you have to run beneath the sterns of one or two starboard tack boats, you will still be ahead of them around the mark because they will have to tack.

The direction of light winds is more likely to vary than in stronger breezes. Most books on yacht racing will tell you always to tack when headed to take advantage of every wind shift. Most sailing books are written for mono-hulls which tack extremely quickly and lose little way. But as we have said before, cats do tack much more slowly and take longer to get moving on the new tack. Therefore every time a cat is headed it is up to the skipper immediately to evaluate the situation and decide whether the shift is only momentary or if it will last for a few minutes. If the wind shift is only temporary, it may be wise not to tack, but to hold course and wait for the breeze to 'lift' once more. Of course, if it looks like holding you must tack immediately. This ability to read the wind shifts is one of the very great skills of cat racing in light airs.

Whatever you do, do not be tempted to chase the breeze right off the course. No matter how it might appear at the time, the law of averages says that each boat in the fleet should have an equal share of the lucky breaks. The best light weather sailors are those who can make the best use of this luck when it comes their way.

Only experience and trial and error will show you how to get the very best out of your own particular boat in light winds, but the correct sheeting of sails is vital. If your boat is sloop-rigged, the jib must be handled very delicately. It should never be sheeted in hard and the leech must be kept free. The jib sheeting position should be moved inboard and aft. If the sail has an adjustable luff, this should be eased, but not let completely free. Some skippers are tempted to sail to windward in light

Lindsay Cunningham and John Buzaglo have Quest II *driving in light airs. John is well forward to keep the lee bow down to utilize maximum waterline length — not a bad idea unless gusty conditions are likely. John keeps low to reduce drag and to give Lindsay a clear view ahead.*

airs with the jib sheeted in hard because they believe they can point higher. This is partly true, but often they do not realize that they could be sailing just as high and a little faster with the jib sheet eased. If the sail is very full it will probably mean sailing to windward with the luff continually breaking. This does not reduce the efficiency of the sail but it does require practice to master the technique. The mainsheet should also be kept comparatively slack and sheeted close to amidships or even slightly to weather if the leech is not inclined to hook. This will depend a great deal on the fullness of the sail. It may also result in some luff flutter developing and the best cure for this is to ignore it!

In many through-batten mainsails the battens can sometimes be reluctant to change tacks when the boat does. The curve in the batten is held by the pressure of the leech of the sail and in very light airs this is greater than the pressure of the wind. We have even seen both of the crew standing on the trampoline, banging and slapping the sail to get it to flop across. If this happens with you, soften your battens and loosen them in the pockets too. Even then the battens may still require some help when tacking. Usually a well-timed shove of the boom to weather will do the trick but it is finding precisely the correct moment to do this that takes practice.

A final point on sailing to windward — use the rules to advantage. If you catch an opponent on starboard and he is a little late in giving way, do not argue; pull off and pass under his stern. You can always protest later or debate the 'you should have's' in the bar after the race. Because, had you screamed 'Starboard!' loud enough and often enough, you would possibly have frightened him into tacking right in front of you. Still breaking the rules of course, but in this case you would lose many boat-lengths in extracating yourself from his wind shadow when, had you run under his stern, the loss would be minimal.

REACHING

All the experts will tell you that on reaching legs you should always head below the mark, sailing an arc to leeward of the straight line course. But how often have you tried this? It takes courage and determination to hold this course once committed, especially when it often appears that the rest of the fleet are doing so much better sailing higher. But it definitely does pay off, even more so in light breezes. If the breeze is varying in

In light airs, resist the temptation to have your crew leap out on the trapeze the moment the weather hull lifts. It is probably only a temporary puff and his movement will only slow the boat down. Former World Tornado Champion, Maurie Davies, has an uncanny touch in light winds.

strength, you should free off in the puffs and sail slightly higher in the light patches.

You must keep your weight well forward to keep the transoms clear of the water and free the sheets even further than you think they should be. This helps counteract the weather helm created by having your weight forward.

'DRIFTER' RACING CAN BE FUN

Boom vangs if properly rigged (and how few are!) can certainly be an advantage, particularly on relatively stiff rigs. The boom vang keeps the leech of the sail firm and minimizes twist. In a bendy rig, however, the vang is often of little value. All that happens is that the tension on the vang is transferred along the boom to the gooseneck, pushing the mast forward which in turn flattens the sail. In boats like the Tornado it is not possible to rig a conventional boom vang effectively because of the short distance between the mast step and the boom. Many Tornados use a separate boom downhaul with the fancy title of a 'go-fast'. This is simply a rope downhaul rigged from about the centre of the boom, down through a fairlead at the gunwale near the chainplate, then to a cleating point. On rounding the weather mark the mainsheet is freed more than usual and the 'go-fast' is hauled in hard and cleated. The mainsheet is then hardened against the downhaul and the resultant forces apply a downward force on the sail.

On a two-man cat in a light breeze the best place for the crew is out on the leeward foredeck. This will keep the boat nicely balanced but it will also enable the crew to support the weight of the jib sheets in his hand and keep the jib perfectly set.

RUNNING

Most high performance cats racing today have developed the technique of downwind tacking. Certainly this is more effective in the classes with high aspect ratio rigs such as the C's, A's and Tornados, but it can also be an advantage in the less sophisticated cats. Generally speaking, the stronger the wind, the more likely that downwind tacking will prove an advantage. This does not mean that it should not be tried in light airs, but that greater skill is required in lighter breezes. Some cats, of course, still carry spinnakers and in most cases it will pay to sail the shortest possible distance to the leeward mark.

Whether you are tacking downwind or heading straight for the mark, it is important that the crew weight is always kept well forward. Not only will this keep the transoms clear of the water but it also has the effect of raking the rig slightly forward. No one seems to be able to explain fully the reason why a boat will sail faster downwind with the rig raked forward, but there is no doubt that it does work.

If your boat has an easily adjustable leech line, this should be hauled on for the free legs of the course. The lighter the wind, the tighter the leech line; even to the point of apparently distorting the sail with 'puckering' along the leech. If the leech line is first hauled in then the mainsheet hardened against it, the effect will be to increase dramatically the fullness of the sail. Make sure, however, that your leech line does run free easily when let go at the leeward mark. And, of course, remember *always* to let the leech line free at the end of each downwind leg of the course. If you forget and haul the mainsheet in for windward sailing with the leech line still tight, you are most likely to break something. Either the line itself will part, or you might even break a batten or two.

In extremely light conditions, drag can sometimes be reduced by raising one rudder blade. This certainly reduces the wetted surface area so theoretically the boat should sail faster. This applies particularly if the rudder blades are very large and the boat is easily steered downwind on only one rudder. If you want to try this on your own boat you will need to have a rudder blade downhaul system that is easily released, and easily applied

Starting in light winds can be tricky, particularly if the line is short or not laid at right angles to the wind. At this start, an A-class has already decided he is too early and is running across the bows of the other boats as he sails down the line. Boat B2/12 appears to have rammed the committee boat. All the other boats bunched near the committee boat seem to be in a hopeless position for a good start. It looks as if KA26 has the best chance of winning the start, or perhaps KA55 if he can get moving quickly enough.

again at the leeward mark. The blade should also be fitted with an uphaul so that you do not have to hang over the stern with your arm thrust into the water trying to lift the rudder blade.

Tacking downwind is an art requiring just as much skill as sailing a cat to windward. Quite apart from the techniques already discussed for getting the boat sailing at her maximum speed when running before the breeze, there are special skills required to master the art of downwind tacking. The reason for downwind tacking is quite simple. Most cats, like most sailing boats, are not especially efficient when sailing dead before the breeze. The true wind and apparent wind is from over the stern and the maximum speed possible will be something less than the speed of the wind over the water. A catamaran, however, will sail much more quickly if headed about thirty or forty degrees toward the wind direction. So much faster, in fact, that it will more than make up for the extra distance sailed in reaching a mark directly to leeward.

Exactly what angle should be sailed to get the very best out of a boat can only be determined by trial and error and by watching other boats sailing in your fleet. But extra speed should not be your sole objective in tacking downwind. It almost goes without saying that the higher you sail, the faster the boat will move through the water. But the higher you sail, the greater the distance that must be covered to reach that mark to leeward. So the art is not necessarily to keep your boat sailing fast (although of course this is important) but to be sailing as fast through the water as your opponents but on a heading that is a little lower than the other boats. You will then have less distance to sail and will reach the mark before them.

Various visual aids can be used to help in determining the most efficient angle

'DRIFTER' RACING CAN BE FUN

for downwind sailing. Perhaps the most simple is pieces of wool about eight inches long attached to the main shrouds approximately four feet above the deck. On cat-rigged boats these can also be used on each forestay. They can be quite useful as a rough guide to the correct sailing angle and in most classes they should be kept streaming at right-angles to the direction of sailing. An extension of this idea is the quite elaborate apparent wind indicators mounted on each bow of the C-class *Quest III*. The sensitive vane not only indicates clearly the direction of the apparent wind but also includes a wire pointer set in such a way that when the vane and the pointer are in line, the optimum angle of sailing has been reached. Some skippers find a deck-mounted compass useful too. There are a number of these on the market, specially designed for this purpose. Perhaps the best use of a compass for downwind sailing is to help in determining the correct angle to sail after gybing rather than the sailing angle after rounding the weather mark.

Finally, a short word about spinnakers. Unfortunately, most modern catamarans no longer carry spinnakers. On the one hand we acknowledge the efficiency of the modern high aspect ratio rig and its ability to sail effectively downwind without the need for a spinnaker, yet on the other hand the departure of the spinnaker from cats is eliminating an incredibly exciting aspect of cat sailing.

When flying a spinnaker in light airs it is even more important to keep the crew movement on the boat down to an absolute minimum. It is completely pointless to jump enthusiastically around the boat in an attempt to hoist the spinnaker quickly on rounding the weather mark. Take your time. Hoist the spinnaker carefully and steadily, making sure that it is not twisted and that all the sheets are free. A topping lift on the spinnaker pole will be essential in light airs and a very light sheet will also help. The few remaining classes that do still carry spinnakers usually favour a very flat cut sail. These are often mitre-cut with a wire or non-stretch tape luff, and are not unlike a very light headsail. Because of this, they can be carried very close to the wind, particularly in drifting conditions. They can be carried on all legs of the course, even to windward! It requires a very skilful crew to tack a spinnaker upwind.

When the sea turns oily like this you can be sure there is no wind on the surface. But Miss Nylex *is leaving a wake so she must be moving, although being sailed badly at the time. Flap angles are incorrectly set and boat should be trimmed down by the bow. Those bumps on the outside of the starboard hull are real but they do look much worse in this picture. The hull was rushed to make trials date and was only faired below the waterline.*

FINISHING

To say that no yacht race is won until the winning boat has cleared the finishing line may sound a little obvious. But this truism applies more in light weather racing than for any other type of conditions.

Light breezes are inclined to be fluky. And when the wind is fluky there is always a chance that one boat will pick up a 'private breeze' missed by the rest of the fleet. So, if you are leading the race, be prepared to defend your position grimly. But if you are behind, do not ever give up the thought of attacking the leaders.

Let us first consider the boat that is leading the fleet to windward and the finishing line. This boat must always attempt to defend her position by keeping between her nearest opponent and the finishing line. If there is more than one boat threatening her leading position and they 'split' by sailing different sides of the course, this will not be possible. Under these circumstances the leader should sail an 'average' course and ensure that every time she tacks she heads toward the finishing line. As the leader approaches the line she should determine which end of the line, if any, is closer and head for that end.

If you are not the leading boat but are within striking distance of the leader you must attack all the way to the line. This does not mean taking silly risks and heading off the course on a 'flyer', but it does mean sailing a different course from the leading boat. If you are being covered, try and break clear, and try to split tacks with the leader rather than match tacks. Implement a tacking duel if you can and if the rest of the fleet are not right on your tail waiting to pounce. You never know, it just might be your turn to benefit from a wind-shift at last.

If you are able fully to rotate your mast and tighten the diamonds, it will greatly increase the power of the rig for upwind sailing in light winds. Although the mast on this Tornado is S-bending somewhat, it is not sufficient to close the slot between main and jib. This boat is sailing very fast in winds of about 10 mph.

IN CONCLUSION

Like all small boat racing, light weather sailing takes practice. But it also requires patience and concentration. The right mental attitude is of vital importance and unless the feeling of prolonged frustration can be overcome, you will never make an expert 'drifter'. If you have done well in a light weather race you will find that your

'DRIFTER' RACING CAN BE FUN

The fully rotated mast on this B-Lion is another example of how a rotating rig should be set for light winds. Unfortunately the crew are not driving the boat as hard as they might.

opponents will accuse you of being lucky. Do not believe them! Convince yourself that it was your own ability that brought about your success.

In extremely light conditions you might wonder how some skippers seem to be able to feel a breeze when, to you, there seems to be no wind at all. The key word is 'feel'. They actually feel the breeze on their face. Next time the breeze drops out and all your wind indicators have given in, try this. Look at the horizon and slowly turn your head through 360 degrees. If you do not screw your head off your shoulders, you will feel the breeze, however slight, on your face.

Finally, what should you do when the breeze comes in? You will see the new breeze on the water and hopefully it will be coming toward you. Watch other boats to determine the direction of the wind and try and sail towards it if you can. Do not be over-zealous in altering all your gear for the fresher wind, although it is not a bad idea to let the leech line go if you are sailing to windward. Bending of the mast, tightening of the foot and luff, altering of sheeting positions, can all be attended to after you have determined the strength of the new breeze and whether it will remain. When the weather has been extremely light and the wind suddenly freshens, it is very easy to be deceived into thinking the wind stronger than it really is. It is the contrast between the two winds that can be so misleading.

So next time the anemometer grinds to a halt and the seas look oily, try and relax, concentrate, be determined and remember that those frustrating 'drifters' can really be fun.

Winning in Strong Winds 6

The ability to race any sailing craft in strong winds successfully is usually only gained from many hours, even years, of sailing experience. Catamaran craft can attain extremely fast speeds in strong winds and the requirements are probably even more demanding for both skipper and crew, compared with single-hulled boats.

The ability to win in these conditions, therefore, is something that can be gained only from racing practice. Whether a one-man or a two-man catamaran is your type of craft, nothing will benefit you more than sailing in strong winds until you are able to handle the craft with the 'sixth sense' that the top skippers in any class have and are able to call on to help them win.

If you analyse the results of all races, you may notice that in strong winds, the more experienced skippers and crews will always seem to win. Some craft benefit from the crew being heavy in body weight, and this factor may have some importance in winning under torrid racing conditions in howling winds. But the more modern racing catamaran designs offer a greater range of tuning advancements, which more than compensate for body weight as a factor in winning. The important points that any skipper and crew needs to bear in mind for heavy winds and rough seas are:

Physical fitness.
Ability to quickly overcome nervous tension, created usually prior to the start.
Ability to set up boat for strong winds.
Absolute single minded attitude to winning.
Experience in racing in strong winds.
Knowledge of just how much the boat can be pushed in torrid conditions without causing damage.

As we have said, being fit is a necessary requirement for both skipper and crew. They both should be quite capable of hanging outboard all the way upwind, and, if necessary, downwind too so that they can get the best out of the boat. Certainly if you are astern of the leaders, you will need to use your body weight to its best advantage, either by swinging from toe straps, trapezing or using a swing plank. And if you are in the lead, you cannot afford to ease up in the physical effort either.

It is a little known fact that ninety-nine per cent of the skippers and crews who arrive at the yacht club to see the wind screaming in the rigging and the waves pounding on the shore immediately get the jitters. It is no fun struggling to rig the boat and launch it. But the majority of crews set themselves the task of rigging and setting up the boat for the conditions regardless of personal feelings. You may never remember a light weather race for long. But the dazzling speeds, flying spray, terrifying moments and relief of finishing (even poorly) in heavy winds will live with you for a long time to come.

Even though you may feel nervous prior to the start, once the starting gun fires you will be so busy concentrating on the job ahead that suddenly, even unconsciously, you will have forgotten all your worries.

WINNING IN STRONG WINDS

And usually the conditions will turn out to be manageable and even enjoyable. So overcome the worrying and concentrate on getting the boat ready to race and win.

Next, the importance of setting up the boat for the prevailing conditions cannot be over-stressed. If you are going to race in strong winds, then you may as well adopt the attitude of 'if it is worth racing, it is worth winning'. This positive approach, aggressive attack, will pay off and can work wonders. Of course, there is no substitute for experience. This applies just as much to strong wind racing as it does to racing under other conditions. Through experience will come the knowledge of just how far you can push the boat to near its maximum limit without causing a severe nosedive, or wrecking the mast, or ripping the sails. Your crew will also learn with experience just where to trapeze from along the gunwale in all conditions. Experience will also determine how much jib sheet to free in a gust or how high or low to hang on the trapeze wire. All these little things when put together, make the crew a winning combination. You will build confidence and confidence breeds success.

SETTING UP THE BOAT

Let us break this down into several areas. We will deal with each item separately for the sake of easy explanation:
Sails and battens.
Mast and boom.
Centreboards and rudders.
The boat.

Sails and Battens. Ideally, you will have set up your sails so that the one set of battens will provide the desired performance and sail shape for most weather conditions. When you are confronted with very strong winds, it will probably be necessary to make changes. The mainsail battens in the lower two-thirds of most catamaran sails will be acceptable but because of the increased pressures on the leech of the mainsail at the peak, it may be necessary to replace at least the top two battens. They should be replaced by battens at least thirty per cent stiffer so that the higher leech pressures are resisted and the leech will remain 'open'. If the leech is allowed to hook, it will result in poorer upwind performance. Some skippers even carry two or three stiffer top battens on the boat and after a test sail or two they will drop the sail and replace the top battens if they feel this is necessary. Only experimentation on your own sails will show you which battens require stiffening for heavy winds.

If you have leech battens in your jib, there should be no need to consider replacing these in strong winds. However, you will need to make sure that they are securely fastened in their pockets as the tremendous whipping forces of the wind can easily flip a jib batten out of the pocket. It may pay to have the jib battens permanently sewn in.

The setting of the sails is very critical in strong winds. Faults that might not be obvious in lighter conditions can become very obvious in strong winds. This can apply to battens, sail cut, sail setting, etc.

Once you have selected and inserted your sail battens, you should set the sails on the spars and forestay with the desired luff and foot tensions for the conditions. However, as this chapter deals with maximum winds for racing, we must stress again the need for a high performance catamaran to be fitted out with luff and foot control systems so that the crew is able to make quick and easy adjustments as the conditions dictate.

Ideally, the mainsail will be hoisted and the luff set at near its maximum tension and likewise for the foot. The jib luff can be tensioned with the luff

Experience as a barefoot water skier or tight-rope walker will help a crew keep his balance and composure in this situation. But the Tornado will keep driving through choppy water even in the most boisterous conditions, as shown in this series of photographs.

This Tornado is reaching across Sydney Harbour in winds gusting at over 30 mph. In the first picture the gust hits and the mainsheet is eased. The boat heels and buries the lee hull in a cloud of spray and the crew bends his knees slightly and leans aft. As the lee hull dives the jib sheet is eased too.

In the second picture, the skipper has pulled away a little to keep the boat sailing at maximum speed and take advantage of the gust. The crew is still beautifully balanced and is driving the boat as hard as he can from out on the trapeze.

In the third picture, a further gust has hit on top of the first, causing some loss of control. The skipper is forced to ease the mainsheet even more, and pull away. The violent move of the boat away to leeward has unbalanced the crew and he has swung aboard near the skipper aft.

WINNING IN STRONG WINDS

adjuster but the foot tension will depend on where the jib is sheeted. The further aft, the tighter the foot. The setting of the jib in relation to the mainsail is very important in all conditions and especially so in strong winds. Keep in mind that the mast, if the rotating type, will tend to 'close the slot' as the mast is rotated for upwind sailing. This can be compensated for by sheeting the jib further outboard. Setting the jib sheet further aft in strong winds will also tend to flatten the foot of the jib and to a degree, lessen the pressure on the jib leech.

The sheeting of the mainsail on the hawse is also extremely important. In strong winds, the mainsail will need to be sheeted further to leeward. You will have to experiment to find the best relative positions for the main and jib. Ideally, the mainsail will be sheeted down hard and cleated. It would then be played on the traveller, letting it out to leeward in the heavy gusts and hauling it back towards the centre as the gust eases. This method requires considerable skill and the skipper will need to be prepared for the extra heavy gust which might put the boat 'on its ear'. Alternatively, if the wind is reasonably constant, you can sheet down and drive to windward, easing the mainsheet in the puffs as required. But strong winds are usually accompanied by strong gusts. This is where experience pays dividends and you will learn which method to use in each set of conditions to get the best advantage from it. Whilst there should be no need for a leech line under heavy conditions and strong winds, it may be required downwind and it would be foolish not to have it ready to use just in case the wind eases. The leech line system which seems best is the one in which the wire leech line runs through nylon slides at the outer end of the sail battens. The type sewn into the leech of the sail is not recommended as it does not always 'ease off' when released and it may retain some unwanted tension.

In setting up your sails for strong winds, remember that it rarely, if ever, pays to flatten out a sail. A flat sail will not usually provide the necessary drive to the boat. At all costs power must be maintained to drive the boat through the seas and to lift to windward as well as driving the boat fast downwind. It is better to maintain power in the rig and set your sail to spill the unwanted power, either by easing the sheet a little or by setting the sails a little more to leeward, or both.

If the winds are so strong that the rig still seems to have too much power, and you are using a rotating mast, then the mast can be de-rotated to the fore-and-aft position. This will allow the top of the mast to bend to leeward, the centre section will bend to windward a little and the slot will be opened between the

Quest III, *perhaps one of the most powerful sailing boats in the world, never appears to be troubled upwind in heavy winds. Crew Graham Ainslie is big and strong, and beautifully balanced here to make the most of his weight. Note the long trapeze wire, strictly for the experts.*

mainsail and jib. This is a drastic action and the subsequent loss of drive from the rig is considerable. But as a last resort it is effective when the wind strength develops to near squall conditions. The boat then becomes manageable and can still be sailed quite efficiently to windward.

The Mast and Boom. The mast is a very important part of the rig of the catamaran. If there are several alternative mast sections available for your class, it will pay to examine which one is most suitable for your prevailing range of conditions. It is useless to select a really stiff mast if it is only good in light winds.

The various control systems also play an important part in altering the mast bending characteristics to suit the conditions. In strong winds, the diamond stays should be tightened a little to protect the mast from the stronger pressures it will need to withstand. It is important to ensure that the diamond spreader is of sound construction, for the load that this piece of equipment is subjected to can be considerable. Other control systems required in strong winds are:

Mast rotation.
Mainsail luff downhaul.
Halyard lock.
Diamond stay adjustment.
Jumper stay adjustment (if used).

The mast should be watertight, if this is possible, otherwise it will fill rapidly with water after a capsize, making righting the boat very difficult. If it is not possible to fully waterproof a mast, it may be possible to seal off part of it. Even filling the mast with foam is an advantage.

The boom usually carries the clew

WINNING IN STRONG WINDS

outhaul, and the leech line system. If a vang is used, its fixing point on the boom will need to be extremely strong. The boom is more important than most of us think. Several top boats have lost races, or been forced to withdraw, because the boom cracked or broke in two. These faults were caused by one of the following:

Boom not strong enough in section.
Bolt holes bored in boom in such a manner that the boom was weakened.
Vang downhaul fixing point on boom was too close to bottom allowing boom to crack.
In a wooden boom, the glue had not set correctly and boom split under strong pressure.

In heavy winds, the failure of a mast is fairly common and is usually due to human error. The diamond spreader attachment point on a mast is often the most common point of breakage. The spreaders themselves can sometimes bend aft at their outboard end. The resultant sudden lack of support breaks the mast in two at the diamond point. The hounds fitting on a mast is also a cause of breakage, usually because it has not been correctly fitted. Even stainless steel shackles have been known to fail on diamond stays. So check regularly all fittings on your mast and boom, especially after a heavy race — or better still, before any heavy weather race.

Centreboards and Rudders. We have dealt thoroughly with rudders and centreboards elsewhere in this book, but in strong wind conditions, they require special consideration. Assuming the shapes are perfect and they are set up correctly, you will have to experiment to determine how far the centreboards need retracting downwind. There is a strong case for retracting the leeward board when on a hard reach, otherwise the

When sailing on a tight reach in fresh winds, it is necessary for the crew to move aft as the wind increases. As the crew moves aft on the trapeze, his body will rise unless he uses the trapeze adjuster to lengthen the wire. Quest III *uses the now common restraining wire to hold the crew aft when reaching.*

pressure generated on the board's leading edge can result in the boat tripping over the centreboard! Both boards need to be fully down upwind. On a reach, a half raised board will help counteract the induced weather helm. You may need no board at all tacking downwind although some skippers prefer just a little.

It is wise to use some sort of centreboard uphaul–downhaul system which can be operated from both sides of the boat. This allows you to make adjustments from either side without the crew

The 20' Yvonne is built for heavy work and these boats are capable of carrying a spinnaker in the wildest weather. The crew sit well aft to keep the bows surfing over the waves.

The pressure exerted on the stocks at the bottom leading edge area is enormous when reaching. It is quite a common sight to see a boat limping home with a broken rudder stock. Resolve now not to let this happen to you.

The tiller system is also important for it must allow the skipper to steer the boat in both very light and heavy winds. If you study the top boats in your class you will find one to suit you. Ensure that the bolts in the linkage of the tiller arms and bars are securely mounted and that the nuts will not unscrew. If necessary, put a drop of quick setting marine glue on the nut to seal it on the bolt.

The Boat. Leaking hulls are bad news. Waterproof your hulls thoroughly to eliminate, as much as possible, any water entry.

The cross members or beams which connect the two hulls must be very firmly secured. In building, ensure that the frames are well made and secure for the pressures are transferred through the beams to the frames in the hulls.

Another important factor to consider for strong winds is that you have hiking devices fitted which will allow you to use your body weight to full advantage. The crew should use an adjustable trapeze wire with a three-to-one purchase system that can be operated to allow him to move forward or aft as conditions allow. There should be foot loops placed along the gunwale at strategic points to provide secure trapezing. The crew may adopt the knotted rope system which loops into a ring on his belt and holds him aft against sudden speed losses. The system is useful in strong winds and it can add immensely to the well-being of the crew. The jib sheet he is handling tends to exert a forward pressure. Toe straps and the knotted rope hold him aft when reaching.

having to move to leeward. It is no fun going to leeward in strong wind conditions! When altering the boards from the weather position with a system, you can leave them to the last moment and then haul them down (or up) when ready.

Finally, remember that the rudder stocks are the most susceptible part of the rudder gear — so they must be strong.

WINNING IN STRONG WINDS

Good cam or clam cleats mounted on the mainbeam, or on the deck should be strategically placed for use by the crew to lock sheets down as required. In strong winds, the crew should wear gloves, and be fit enough to hold the jib sheet so that instant release is possible. You may need to add ratchet blocks to the jib sheet system to aid him. Your body weight may be moved further aft in strong winds, especially downwind, so that the bows are kept high.

The trampoline should be lashed so tightly that little flap is permitted. A floppy trampoline, under strong wind conditions will blow upwards and create a most undesirable aerodynamic effect. The trampoline should have water outlets placed in areas where water will readily collect — for example, around the position where the crew's feet are placed. On a plywood bridgedeck floor holes cut to drain water should be the maximum allowed. These should be placed near the hull and not in the centre of the flooring where water will rarely collect.

Make sure you use only top quality lashing with a trampoline. Inferior or old lashing will fray and break under the strain of racing in strong winds.

Now we come to the racing of the boat. The areas we will cover are:
The start.
Windward leg.
Reaching.
Tacking downwind.
Running.

Two on the trapeze makes the Stingray an exciting cat in fresh breezes. Teamwork between skipper and crew is vital, especially when the lee bow starts to disappear under foam. When this happens the crew must start easing the jib sheet to prevent a nose-dive.

Many of your competitors will tear up and down the line while they wait for the gun at the ten-minute signal. But it is important to position yourself in an area where you can see and, if possible, hear the gun fire so that you or your crew can get the time set on a watch. The five-minute gun will then give you the opportunity of checking the precise time, so make certain that you are in a good position for this too.

You would be better off to sit to windward and not too far away from the starting boat so that your drift (allowing also for tide, if any) carries you towards and past the committee boat outside the line. If you can furl your jib so that it is not thrashing around in the strong wind, so much the better. Fully battened mainsails

Cat sailing at its very best. With flat seas and fresh winds this Tornado is flying to windward. The crew is flat out on trapeze but the skipper would not be able to maintain delicate control when swinging out this far.

can be fairly docile in strong winds when the boat is luffed to. Once your starting time is established, work out the best position for your start. With the firing of the five-minute gun, you should be ready to move into the starting position. Be wary of a large concentration of boats at the starboard end of the line and try to get a good start at top speed with clear wind along the line. But do not sacrifice a windward position if you feel there is a good chance of starting further to windward. Remember that jockeying around for a good position which means tacking prior to the start can be quite dangerous in these conditions. You will need to try to make up your mind as early as possible on where you should be starting across the line. An accident or a rule infringement in a bunch of boats in strong winds might end the race for you.

Usually, the top boats are quietly

WINNING IN STRONG WINDS

sitting, luffed up, right up to within the last minute. They then slowly jockey towards the line and really go for full power in the final fifteen seconds or so. In strong winds, if you are too early, you really are in big trouble. The other boats are not going to open up a space for you and you might cause a lot of damage. If you have to bear away, you will be increasing your speed rapidly and you must have clear space to leeward. Otherwise, you will just have to luff sharply and sit it out until the boats ahead of you are sheeted in and have crossed the line. As skipper, you will be very busy, so your crew should quietly call the countdown from his watch. You can call back to him when you want him to sheet on the jib. Try and keep your wind clear to windward, and try not to be put in a position where a leeward boat can luff you.

During the last few seconds, sheet in and pick up speed. If you are too slow in moving, the boats to windward will sail over you and leave you wallowing in the disturbed air. If you get a good start, your windward side will be clear ahead and you should be off with full speed. With disturbed air, if you started down the line a little, you will find it very difficult to tack to get away into a clear wind. You may be forced to sail on until an opportunity opens up for a smart tack.

Once you have started you must quickly settle down to the job in hand — that of getting to the windward mark first, or at least in the first bunch of boats. Do not throttle your boat speed by pinching. But if the boat is heeling too much in the gusts, open up the jib slot by sheeting the jib more to leeward. It may also pay to sheet the mainsail further to leeward on the traveller. Keep the boat moving fast at all costs, even if it means bearing off a little to do so.

There is no prize for 'pinching' in strong winds — boat speed is what counts. The only time that you may have to pinch a little is if a boat is coming up astern and you wish to protect your position. You might then point a little higher just to get lifted to windward. But keep in mind that speed is all important and go for it with all your energy. Hang out hard in these conditions to use your weight. Your crew may cleat the jib sheet but he must remember to recover it before you tack. Call out clear instructions to him so he knows what you want to do. If you are cleating the mainsail, be

The halyard lock has many advantages, but one disadvantage is the fixed position of the mainsail on the mast. Some classes allow the main to be lowered on the mast for heavy winds, greatly reducing the heeling movement of the rig. This boat is Peter Bolton's Yvonne class Fran, *a noted heavy weather performer.*

The 12' Kitty has a remarkable sail carrying ability. There is a pair of hulls somewhere under all that spray.

wary of hard gusts. If you can, try to hold it in your hand rather than cleat it. And remember always to uncleat it before you tack. Your crew will probably find that he should trapeze a little further aft in these conditions so that the bows are lifted to take the higher waves. The skipper may also be hanging further aft than normal, too.

If you find the weather boat is pointing

WINNING IN STRONG WINDS

higher, you may need to re-sheet the jib, bringing it inboard a little to close the slot. And you may need to sheet the mainsail in a more central position. You can also lift your boat to windward with each strong gust in a series of 'lifts'. This may slightly reduce your boat speed but can assist you in getting higher to windward when required. Try and get the full amount of performance out of the boat at all costs. Force yourself to concentrate on sailing the boat fast. If the boat is still tending to lift in the puffs, it may pay to ease the mainsheet a little. Mast rotation is important and today's high performing catamarans tend still to use considerable mast rotation, even in strong winds. But you might find that less rotation will pay dividends, opening up the jib slot and allowing the mast to bend off at the peak.

If you are racing in big seas, try and steer over them. With practice, you will find that you can sheet in on the main, lift the windward hull a little higher and sail over a big wave with minimum fuss. But try to keep the boat fairly level at all other times. In huge seas, you may find the technique of a slight zig-zag course is better: point the boat slightly into the coming sea and bear off slightly as you reach the crest. The crew may need to move further aft still in really large waves to lift the bows. Keep the boat 'alive', with speed your main concern. Keep watching your sails and keep watching the seas. Your crew can keep you in touch with the positions of the other boats in the fleet. But he must be using his weight to the best advantage. Even though you can help him by leaning out, do not get too enthusiastic about hiking yourself. You need to be able to watch the seas and the sails too and your steering ability and that of sheeting the mainsail is more important than hanging over the side by your toes.

Tacking a catamaran in these rugged conditions is often not easy. You need to select the best time to do it. In big seas, try and tack the boat on the crest of a wave rather than in a trough. The boat will respond more quickly and, as it tacks through the eye of the wind, the next wave will hit the new 'weather' hull and help the boat about. Do not tack with the jib and/or the mainsheet locked or cleated, but keep the pressure on the sheets by hand throughout the tack. On the new tack, you can sheet in the slack quickly and be smartly about and off on your new course. Try not to tack more often than is absolutely necessary in strong winds. Go for the long beats to windward if this is at all reasonably possible. Naturally, if you are involved in covering an opponent or pressing him, you will want to use tactics. If you and your crew are good at tacking in strong winds, you can quickly resort to a tacking duel and you may force the other fellow to put in a bad tack which will quickly give you a decided advantage.

One point to remember in tacking is that it can pay to point the boat slightly higher on the new tack for a short time until you get your gear and yourselves sorted out. This will help your crew to clip onto the trapeze and get outboard faster. If you can cleat the mainsail for short moments, you might do so now and help your crew haul in the jib sheet with your free hand. Your crew will know that he must always hang on to the jib sheet. If he falls overboard, he must have something to help him get back on board quickly and will not be lost astern.

When you round the weather mark, settle down first and determine your course. Get your own weight right aft as far as possible. Your crew may even be straddling you, with a foot each side of your body as he hikes out from the trapeze. Set your traveller to leeward and sheet in the mainsail. Get the boat on course fast and keep that speed up to cover ground to the next mark quickly. In the gusts, bear away to leeward to maintain speed, easing the sheets slightly. Haul them in and round up in the lulls. This action will maintain higher speeds and get you downwind fast. Keep watching the leeward bow and be ready to take action if it starts to nose in. In strong winds, the best boats will be driving along at top speed and often will take a slight nosedive. Do not be afraid to force the boat along. But quick recovery action is required to stop the situation worsening.

As skipper, your big opportunity to hike outboard hard is on the reach when all body weight is valuable to keep the boat trimmed. When racing downwind in high seas, you will need to work the helm to take advantage of the seas and use them to push the boat along.

You may have to steer more of a zig-zag course, running down the larger waves and luffing in the calmer areas. But remember to use the gusts to get to leeward of the rhumb line and the lulls to sharpen up and maintain speed. Your crew will be working the jib constantly, even if only slightly, to keep it trimmed. As you bear off in a gust, he should ease the sheet, and as he feels you coming up again he must sheet in.

At the gybe mark, get your crew inboard at the last possible moment. Free your traveller for the gybe and send your crew across as you begin the gybe. Follow him smartly as the gybe takes effect. Sheet in quickly and get the boat on course fast. Catamarans are fairly docile creatures in a gybe situation, even in very strong winds. Do not let your mainsheet off too far, otherwise the boom will tend to 'sky'. If you have no vang system you could be in trouble, so control the gybe through the mainsheet. On the next reach, continue to push the boat

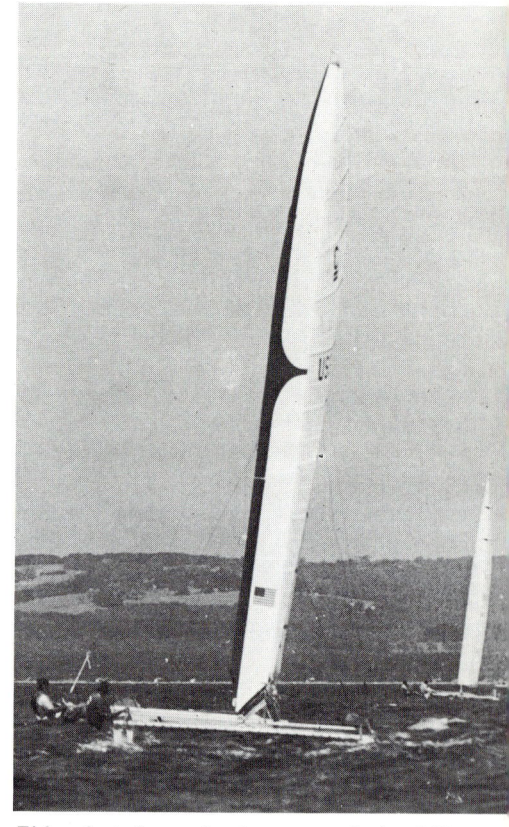

This shot from dead astern of the US challenger, Weathercock, *highlights their major rig control problems. Upper leech of the sail is falling away to leeward completely destroying the effectiveness of the rig.* Quest III, *in the distance, has her leech standing straight.*

hard and fast. Round the mark steadily and steer the boat slightly to leeward of the course. This allows you time to sheet in and get on course fast.

By now, you will be enjoying the race, even anticipating the next leg and working out the best side of the course to sail.

WINNING IN STRONG WINDS

And when you do fall over, this is not the way to right the boat. The crew attempting to climb up the bridgedeck will very quickly have the boat upside down. The skipper at the stern is not helping much either. When a cat capsizes, one of the crew should immediately move around the boat and sit on the lower centreboard. The other crew should not attempt to climb on the boat, but should remain in the water until he has worked his way around to the bottom of the boat.

Remember the importance of practice for any conditions of wind; and watch those who sail well and often finish well. Prepare your boat for rugged conditions before the race and prepare yourself. Your heavy weather race will then be more enjoyable and soon become more rewarding.

Tuning for Faster Sailing 7

The tuning of any racing sailing boat is usually highly complex. It is a combination of many, many factors, all interrelated, and all totally important to the end result — a race-winning boat. In fact, tuning is such an involved subject that it is difficult for us to know where to start, and how to go about making suggestions that might be tried in your own racing. If in this book you find just one idea that proves effective, then this chapter has been worth while.

However, before we look at the various aspects of tuning a racing catamaran, there are a number of comments and observations we would like to make. These points are not necessarily directly related to the actual tuning of a boat but we believe them to be of sufficient importance to be included in this chapter.

1 **Experience.** There is no substitute for experience. All the tuning hints in the world, a vast wardrobe of costly sails, imported gear, a professionally built and fitted boat, a world champion crew — none of these can replace racing experience for a skipper of a racing cat. And although racing experience is of the utmost importance, it is making use of this experience that really counts. There are many very experienced catamaran sailors racing today who never seem quite able to get their boats sailing well enough to challenge the leaders in their fleet. Often this is because they have failed to make the best use of their wealth of experience. Why then, you might ask, is it not uncommon to find among the leading skippers, a young and relatively inexperienced cat sailor? This is simply because these fellows have the wonderful ability to make the very best use of their limited experience, and the ability to take advantage of the experience of others.

2 **Practice.** Practice is not the same as experience. Practice is specific, experience is general. By practice we mean the development of your sailing technique; the perfection of teamwork with your crew; the development of speed and smoothness in tacking and the speed and efficiency in the way you use your gear. Call it tuning the crew if you like, but by any name, it too is of vital importance to your boat's performance.

3 **Boat and Crew Weight.** When it comes to making a catamaran sail fast, it will always be much easier with a light boat and a heavy crew than with a heavy boat and light crew, even if the all-up weight is the same. If your class rules stipulate a minimum weight and you are serious about your racing, make sure that your boat is right down to this weight. For example, in the Tornado class where a minimum weight boat is not absolutely essential, all the top boats are within fifteen pounds of the 280-pound minimum. Crew weight is less critical, because the weight is moveable. Some of the very best light weather boats have

TUNING FOR FASTER SAILING   97

This is a classic shot of Maurie Davies' World Champion Tornado, Windsong, *being superbly well sailed to windward on Sydney Harbour. Crew Ian Ramsay is working hard and Maurie is nice and comfortable and completely in control.*

D

the heaviest all-up crew weight and conversely, some of the best heavy weather performers are relatively light.

4 **Sails.** Sailmakers are blamed more often for more racing failures than any other person or outside factor. Yet, very rarely are they to blame. Good sails are essential on any high performance racing boat, but so often we have seen good sails become mediocre sails because of poor handling or setting by the crew. Most new sails from a reputable sailmaker will be good, particularly if this sailmaker has had experience and successes in your class. But no two sails are exactly the same. Because they are hand-made there will be minor differences that must be taken into account when setting them for the first time. Never rely on a new sail replacing an old one without the need to make alterations to the variable gear such as battens, mast bend, leech line tension, luff tension, sheeting position, etc. When you buy a new sail, always give it a fair chance to prove its worth. If you do not win your first race with a new sail, or your second race, or even your third, resist the temptation to rush back to the sailmaker to complain or have him make alterations. Try and determine, first, whether or not you are making the best possible use of your new sail.

No matter how good a sail might be and how attached you might become to it, it will not last forever. The life of a sail varies from class to class and the amount of heavy use it has. A sail used in light winds will always outlast one used mainly in strong winds. And, of course, the type of cloth used will influence the life of the sail. In our experience, a mainsail on a mono-type cat, such as the Australis, or one on a class like the Tornado, can be expected to be reaching the end of its useful racing life towards the end of the second season of regular hard racing. A headsail will be permanently distorted much more quickly. So much so that in all the sloop-rigged cat classes that enjoy keen competitive racing, the top skippers will buy a new jib for every sailing season.

So the message is, stay with the better-known sailmakers, particularly those experienced in your class, and unless there is an obvious error in the way the sail has been cut or made, persevere with the sail without alteration.

5 **Below the Water.** It is rather stating the obvious to say that the finish on the underwater surface of the hulls, rudders and centreboards must be near perfect to win a race in the big league. Yet, surprisingly enough, this aspect of boat preparation is often overlooked, even by a few of the better skippers. It is true that most boats will get a complete paint job during the winter months, and if this is done correctly, it will include filling of all the scratches, chips and cracks plus sanding with fine grit wet-and-dry paper and the application of at least two coats of a marine gloss paint. If possible it would be preferable to have the hulls spray-painted as this will give a harder and brushmark-free finish.

Fibreglass hulls should be thoroughly cleaned and all the rough spots repaired with a suitable resin filler. Then the surface should be polished with a special fibreglass polish that is readily available. This seems like the standard procedure for any racing sailboat, and so it is. The result is a fair, smooth finish for the start of the sailing season.

However, many boat owners neglect the hull finish on the boat during the season and, after all, most of the important races are well after the season has started. Because of the nature of a catamaran, the bulk and comparatively

TUNING FOR FASTER SAILING

heavy weight, the hull finish is likely to deteriorate during the season regardless of how careful you might be in launching and beaching your boat. So make sure that you inspect the underwater finish of your hulls regularly, particularly before and during an important regatta, continuing to fill and polish out any blemishes that may be found.

If the finish on the hulls is important, then the finish (and shape) of the rudders and centreboard is equally so. Rudders easily get knocked about, chipped and scratched, and do require constant attention. Also check your rudder blades for shape regularly, especially after hot, sunny weather. Wooden rudder blades can easily warp in a hot sun and this completely ruins their aerofoil efficiency. In fact, if your rudder blades are often exposed to hot sunlight, it is wise to make them out of either hardwood or laminated softwood and then sheath them in fibreglass. Painting them white or a similar light and highly reflective colour will also help minimize the warping problem. The same comments apply for dagger centreboards. The big advantage with the swinging centreboards such as those in the Tornado, is that they are stored in the case well out of harm's way when the boat is ashore. They are also protected from exposure to the hot sun. The major disadvantage with them is that they tend to be almost forgotten and rarely examined by the skipper for chips or flaws in the shape. At the high speeds sailed by most cats a painted wooden centreboard is very easily damaged by striking a floating object. Even something quite small like an empty beer can will cause damage, and if this happens during the turmoil of a race it is likely that the skipper will not even notice hitting something, or will forget about it after the race.

So, remember, be most meticulous

An earlier shot of Maurie Davies when he still used a wire hawse. Windsong *was not racing when this was taken so do not be too critical of the way the main is sheeted. But it is interesting to note that although the boom is not strapped down and the sail has developed twist, the excellent battens are still holding the leech firm.*

about maintaining the smooth finish on your hulls and carry out regular inspections of your centreboards and rudder blades.

6 **Mental Approach.** In any class of catamaran, or any sailing boat for that matter, the yachtsmen who regularly perform well and win the races that really

One of the first Australis to be built with a straight main beam and no dolphin striker. The mast is misbehaving a little, especially as conditions are fairly light.

TUNING FOR FASTER SAILING

This lightly rigged open B-class suffers from a common problem. Her mast is S-bending in spite of the diamond stays and jumper. The mast appears to be rotated at about 90° and a little less rotation might pull it straight.

count at major regattas have a mental approach to their sailing that is different from most others in the fleet. This difference is most difficult to describe in specific terms and will not necessarily be the same with each top helmsman, but it is certainly a very real factor in yacht racing. It is a skill essential to winning but one that is not easily acquired.

A racing yachtsman must have complete confidence in his own ability and must know in his own mind that he has the capability to win the race. Without this confidence, a race will be lost before the start, regardless of how well he has his boat moving. He must also have complete confidence in the way he (and his crew) has set up the boat for each particular race. Soon after the start of any race, most skippers find that they have a nagging doubt about the way they have prepared the boat. 'Should we have used the flat jib?' 'Are those battens too stiff?' 'We should have raked the mast.' And so on! The very good skipper also has these same thoughts but he is able totally to eliminate them from his mind and concentrate only on getting the best from his boat with the gear as it is.

Every racing skipper will make some mistakes during a race. Sometimes these are quite minor and will not influence the boat's overall performance. On the other hand, some mistakes can mean time or distance lost and will be very irritating. A slow tack, overstanding a mark, a tangled or trailing sheet, or failure to cover an opponent are the sort of small errors which, apart from being costly, can upset the concentration of a racing skipper. Yet the brilliant helmsman has such a single-mindedness about winning the race, that he is able to overlook the small problems at the time and concentrate wholly on sailing fast.

Of course, confidence alone will not win races for you, and over confidence is perhaps more of a handicap than a lack of confidence. Also, confidence is something that should not be talked about very often. It means nothing to loudly boast in the club house before the race, 'My boat is really tramping, watch us go today!' If this is the way you really feel, keep it to yourself, then allow yourself the luxury of a little smugness after the race when you have shown the fleet your foaming sterns.

We cannot hope to pass on through these pages a winning mental attitude to catamaran racing. But we can try to give 'mental attitude' the degree of emphasis that we feel it deserves. In our opinion it is the most important single ingredient in a race-winning combination. Races have been won in the past by heavy boats or boats with a rough finish, or one rudder, or with faulty sails gear or equipment. But races will never be won by a skipper who has a negative mental attitude to his sailing.

Stop for a moment and think long and hard about your own mental approach to your cat racing. Where does your own attitude lie in relation to others? Is there anything you can do to be more positive and confident in your own ability? Keep working on it. There is more to be gained here than can ever be achieved through a new sail or a more bendy mast.

So much for our preliminary comments. Let us now look at the actual tuning processes for an average racing catamaran. Although the tuning of the boat is a combination of many factors, we will deal with each department on the boat separately. These fall into four broad categories:

Underwater — rudders and centreboards.
Deck fittings, gear and equipment.
Mast and rigging, including the boom.
Sails — mainsail, jib and battens.

RUDDERS AND CENTREBOARDS

Some cats have only a single central centreboard whilst the more modern ones have twin boards. Some centreboards are of the dagger type and others pivot and retract into the centrecase.

Rudders vary in type too. Some are wooden, some are aluminium. Some classes have a fixed rudder blade whilst others have a dagger rudder blade. By far the most common type of rudder, however, is the swinging blade type.

Whatever the rudder and centreboard set-up on your boat, it will perform precisely the same function and have as much influence over the boat's performance as the one on a different class of cat.

We all know that, basically, the centreboard is there to prevent the boat moving sideways through the water, and the rudder is to steer the boat. This is of course true, but there is much more to it than this. Both the centreboards and rudders have a very major influence over the balance of the boat. By balance we mean the degree of weather or lee helm a boat might have when sailing to windward. In fact, some skippers wrongly believe that it is only the centreboard and mast rake that can influence a boat's balance. This is not so. Other factors, such as the fullness of the sail, leech tension, sheeting positions, crew weight and rudder blade angle, will all play their part.

Let us look at the centreboards first. Basically, the further the centreboard is moved forward, the greater will be the weather helm, and vice versa. Many of the popular one-design classes do not have the facility to alter the position, fore and aft, of the centreboards and some skippers find this frustrating. In most cases the position of the boards has been well planned and tested by the designer, so your objective should be to try to get the boat performing at her best, without the need to move the centreboards.

However, minor adjustments can often be made. In a cat with a dagger board the platecase is usually built a little longer than the actual depth of the board itself. The board is then positioned by using some form of packing in the case. This works fine provided the packing is well fastened, will not damage the leading and trailing edges of the board, and the rubber or fairing on the bottom of the

TUNING FOR FASTER SAILING

At first glance the rig on these two Arrows being sailed to windward will seem to be similar. Now look more closely. 230 has a pair of spreaders from the mast to the side stays, plus a single jumper stay high enough to clear the jib leech. 150 also has a pair of spreaders from mast to side stays but they are a foot or so lower than 230. If you lay the page down and look up along each mast you will see a difference in their bend characteristics. 230's mast is quite straight to the jumper, then the bend is sudden with the upper section also fairly straight. 150's mast has a beautiful even curve from step to mast head.

case is not interfered with. By shaping the packing, the boards can even be raked aft with this set-up. Incidentally, never ever rake the leading edge of a centreboard forward of vertical.

On boats with a swinging board, the position of the board is almost always fixed. It is true that the actual centre of effort of the board can be moved aft by swinging the board aft. But as this partly raises the board it will also reduce its efficiency. This is strictly a compromise and should only be tried when all else has failed to reduce weather helm. Those classes with a single central swinging centreboard do have the facility to move the board fore and aft slightly and to rake the board without greatly reducing the effective area. For some reason, cats with this type of centreboard system always seem to sail better to windward with the board raked aft about ten or fifteen degrees off vertical. This seems to be the case regardless of other tuning factors on the boat.

Our advice on centreboards is, therefore, to leave them well alone. In most classes the designer knew what he was doing when he positioned the centrecase and the board. When racing upwind, the centreboard should always be fully lowered. The only exception is for classes that still have the single central board, and these should be raked slightly aft.

The rudder, however, can have far greater influence over the balance of the boat and ultimately in her performance, both upwind and down. The position of the rudder blade, fore and aft, when fully lowered is absolutely critical. If the blade is allowed to rake only slightly aft of its normal position, quite fierce weather helm can be induced, especially downwind. If the blade is forward of the ideal position the helm will be lacking in that all-important 'feel' and the rudders will be inclined to stall out in violent manoeuvres.

As a starting point we would suggest that you set up your rudder blades so that when fully lowered, the leading edge is at right-angles to the true water line of the boat. Note that this is not the same as being at right-angles to the bottom of the boat or the keel line. It is most important that both the rudder stock and the blade be so constructed that they permit the free movement up and down of the blade but do not allow any sloppiness whatsoever when the blade is locked down. Any wear in the pivot hole in the blade will make the blade sloppy on the pivot bolt and this must not be tolerated. Whatever system you use to lower the rudder blade and hold it down, it must be positive and not allow the blade to creep up during a race.

By far the best method of pulling a rudder blade down and holding it there is to use a heavy cord or wire around the top of the blade and out through a sheave at the aft end of the tiller. The downhaul is pulled towards the skipper to lower the blade and then securely fastened on the tiller. The downhaul system should include at least six inches of very heavy shock cord to keep the blade firmly butted against its stop. The shock cord will also allow the blade to move in the stock in the event of hitting something in the water, thus preventing serious damage.

When the rudder blade is lowered, the top of the leading edge of the blade will butt against the lower part of the rudder stock. This is what limits the downward movement of the rudder blade and the point which determines the precise rudder blade angle. With frequent, and sometimes violent, raising and lowering of the rudder blades, this point of contact often becomes worn or bruised or, worse, the top of the blade itself becomes damaged. Wear at this point will almost certainly result in a change in the angle of the rudder blade, and because it happens gradually over a number of races, the skipper is often completely unaware of it. If you find that your own boat has lost some of the 'feel' or helm sensitivity that it had a few weeks before, the rudder blade angle is one of the first things to check. A very slight change in rudder blade angle can have a marked effect on performance, and the deeper the rudder blade is, the greater the effect.

Boats with fixed rudders or blades of the dagger type give less opportunity for moving the effective area of the rudders fore and aft. However, with the dagger blade system, it is possible to vary the angle of rake by using packing, provided, of course, the class rules permit this.

If your class rules permit, there is a lot of experimenting that can be done in tuning your boat by varying the area of the rudder blades. A basic principle is that smaller blades will increase the weather helm of the boat, and larger or deeper rudder blades will improve the pointing ability but may induce some lee helm. Of course, small blades will be stronger, and large blades will increase the total surface area, resulting in increased drag. There is no simple answer that would apply to a variety of classes of catamaran so we will not try to give one. But if you are handy at making rudders, there is a lot of fun to be had and know-

TUNING FOR FASTER SAILING 105

In this series of four photographs we have attempted to show the effect that mast rotation can have on the shape of the sail and in the way the mast itself bends. At the time these were taken the boat was of course on the beach. Unfortunately there was very little wind so the changes in shape evident here need to be magnified for a sailing situation.
In the top left hand picture the mast is set fore and aft. The head of the mast is starting to fall away to leeward and the luff of the sail is very flat. As the mast is rotated through to about 80° in the bottom right hand picture, the top moves to windward and fullness increases.

ledge to be gained in experimenting with rudder blade size, shape and angle.

FITTINGS, GEAR AND EQUIPMENT

Some details of fittings and equipment have been covered elsewhere but, as this is a chapter on tuning a cat, the fittings and gadgetry on the boat cannot be overlooked as these play a major role in the tuning function.

Much of the skill in tuning a racing sailing boat comes from being able to make adjustments on the boat quickly, accurately and confidently, in order to take advantage of the prevailing conditions. Therefore, whilst the gear must be kept as simple as possible, it must be efficient, strong and reliable. All sheaves must run freely and every slide on every track must be free to move without the need to apply heavy-handed persuasion. Sheets and wires must be checked constantly for wear and replaced *before* they start to give trouble. Both cam cleats and clam cleats will wear after a time and allow a rope under load to slip. These must be replaced about one race before this starts to happen. A few drops of oil regularly applied to most movable gear will usually work wonders, and make the gear last longer too.

If you find that any piece of equipment used on the boat during a race starts to give trouble, or will only work if used a 'special way', then fix it, modify it or get rid of it altogether and replace it with something else. If you persevere with just one item of faulty equipment on the boat, you ought to question your own attitude to racing. Faulty gear should never be tolerated.

The amount of gear required on a racing cat will vary from class to class, and to some extent is dependent on the rules of each particular class. This can range from the relatively basic items on a class such as the Australian Quickcat to the rather more complex boats like the Tornado and the International C-class. The important consideration is to plan your boat so that you have just enough gear to make all the necessary alterations during a race, and eliminate all the gear that is rarely used.

Before looking at those items that we believe it is essential to be able to adjust, there is one comment that applies to all adjustable gear. That is, *all adjustable gear must have some form of calibration.* Whether this is simply numbers painted on the deck or the mast, coloured thread in a sheet, strips of coloured adhesive tape or marks of another kind, is not important. But a calibration of some form is essential if ever you are to duplicate the way the boat is set up from one race to another. The adjustable gear which particularly requires a method of calibration includes the following:

Mainsheet traveller.
Luff downhaul for main and jib.
Jib halyard tension.
Main foot outhaul.
Leech line.
Jibsheet position, in and out, fore and aft.
Mast rotation.

Most top racing cats should be able to adjust the following items for tuning while sailing:

Mainsheet traveller.
Luff tension, on all sails.
Clew outhaul.
Leech line.
Jib sheeting position.
Mast rotation (if class rules allow).
Diamond stay tension (if class rules allow).

Other items, to be adjusted ashore, include:

Mast rake.
Centreboard position.
Sail battens.
Rudder blade angle.

TUNING FOR FASTER SAILING

Two views of the upper section of Quest III's *1972 rig. The two plywood struts on the top battens helped control the shape of the upper sail. The small pointer near the letter 'K' was one of* Quest's *many indicators. When the sail touched this point, mast rotation was at its maximum for efficient downwind sailing.*

Fitting location.

To return for a moment to the need to have some form of calibration or indicator on your adjustable gear, there are two basic reasons why this is important.

Firstly, it is not good enough to set up the boat with everything 'about right'. Can you be certain that the luff tension is the same as the last time you raced in similar conditions? And how much leech line is enough? You ought to know exactly how you had your boat set up last time you raced and be able to duplicate every setting or make changes in precise terms.

The second reason is more applicable to two-man boats. If your gear is calibrated it will provide a basis for communication between the skipper and his crew. The skipper will be able to request alterations in precise terms rather than vague suggestions. For example, he can ask for the mainsail luff to be tensioned to 'position five', or moved from 'blue' to 'red'. It matters not what the markings are, only that they are there and readily understood by both members of the crew.

So, having reached a point where we understand that a certain amount of adjustable gear is essential for the tuning of a racing cat, and that the various settings be clearly marked, let us now look at the effect that some of these

The Australian C, Helios, *showed lots of promise in the 1972 selection trials but she was unable to prevent her sail from developing excessive 'twist', clearly evident in this picture.*

adjustments will have on the boat's racing performance.

MAST AND RIGGING

On a racing cat the mast, together with the rigging, is perhaps the most critical factor in the tuning of the boat. It is certainly equal to, if not more important than, the sails. There are so many variables with a mast and rig that it is always difficult to strike the happy combination without a great deal of experimentation.

The first variable is the flexibility of the bare spar itself. Although some classes still persevere with wooden spars, the aluminium mast section has almost completely taken over. Some class rules are quite precise about what extruded mast sections may or may not be used, yet others allow quite a wide choice. Even in the classes where the rules are quite specific there will still be room for some degree of variation to suit individual tastes.

Basically, there are two ways of going about obtaining an aluminium mast for a catamaran. You can either go to a professional spar maker and purchase one complete 'off the rack', or you can purchase a bare spar length from an aluminium supplier and complete the mast yourself. With the second method you could have the mast finished and fitted professionally but it would probably cost a little more this way. The way you choose to go about it will depend largely on the depth of your pocket and your skill in making up a mast from the bare extruded length.

Apart from saving money, there is no doubt that by obtaining your own mast length and finishing it yourself (or with assistance), you are more likely to get exactly what you want.

If you choose to buy a fully professional mast then we can only suggest that you look at the masts on the leading boats in your fleet and go to the same supplier.

If, on the other hand, you decide to assemble your own mast (and this is much more fun) we can offer a few suggestions.

The first thing to realize is that no two mast lengths will be exactly the same. It is true that some will be similar but there will be some variation, even if only slight, in a quantity of mast lengths all from the one batch from the one extruder. The hardness of the aluminium may vary, the wall thickness may also vary by one or two thousandths of an inch. You will almost certainly find that there is a weight difference, sometimes as much as ten per

TUNING FOR FASTER SAILING

Bill Hollier's C-class, Red Roo, used the radial hawse to strap the boom down effectively and hold the leech steady.

cent, but more often four or five per cent. All of these variables will influence the flexibility of the finished spar.

You might also find that a section suitable for your class is available from more than one supplier, and although the nominated dimensions and weight of these sections might appear to be almost identical, often on close examination they prove to have quite different characteristics.

When you purchase a mast length we suggest that you check it on five counts before you take delivery.

1. Make sure that the length is straight.
2. Make sure that it is not twisted.
3. Make sure that it is not dented or kinked.
4. Weigh it.
5. Check its flexibility.

A simple check for flexibility is as follows. Balance the mast length on a fulcrum approximately twelve inches off a flat surface. Ask someone to push one end down to the ground, and then measure the distance from the raised end down to the ground. Using this method you can very quickly check through a batch of mast lengths to find one of the desired flexibility. As a double check you

Not only is the rudder blade angle extremely important for the correct balance of the boat, but the mechanism that holds the blade down must do its job too. Here Max has his hands full controlling his Tornado on a fairly brisk reach. He will certainly need to get that blade down again for the windward leg.

should test the mast lying on one side first, then flip it over and repeat for the other side. The reading should, of course, be the same. As a general rule, a mast that is more flexible in sideways bend will also be more flexible in fore-and-aft bend, and vice versa.

Whether you should be seeking a mast which is comparatively stiff, comparatively flexible, or about average, is something you will only find out with experience, experimentation and by careful observation of the winning boats in your fleet. However, the following pointers can be taken as a general rule:

If you prefer full sails, select a more flexible mast.

If your sails will be relatively flat, have a stiff mast.

If you race mostly in wind over fifteen knots, choose a flexible mast.

If the winds are light, choose a stiff one.

TUNING FOR FASTER SAILING

A light crew will need a more flexible mast than a heavy crew.

Some classes permit the upper section of the mast to be tapered while, for cost and simplicity reasons, other classes outlaw this practice. The theoretical purpose of tapering the upper section of the mast is to allow a greater degree of flexibility in this region.

Tapering is very simply achieved by cutting a 'V' piece out of the mast, closing up the section and welding along the cut. However, the peculiarities of welding aluminium are such that the weld itself is often harder than the surrounding metal and this can tend to compensate for the metal removed in the tapered area. Even if the flexibility of the upper section is unaffected by tapering, the mast will look a little better if tapered towards the top. Certainly on a Tornado there is no noticeable difference in the bend characteristics of the upper section of a tapered mast when compared with one of the same section untapered.

In most of the one-design classes of catamaran the height of the hounds on the mast above the deck is tightly controlled, and so too is the amount of standing rigging. Let us assume that you have set up the mast with all the necessary bits and pieces as allowed by your class rules and as used by the better boats in your fleet. It is likely that in the area of tuning, your mast will have a set of diamond stays, possibly a jumper stay, and a rotation control lever. It should also contain a facility for tensioning the sail luff, although this is sometimes fitted to the boom. The tension of the diamond stays and jumper stay will also be adjustable, either by turnbuckle or worm screw.

We have now established that for tuning purposes we can either increase or decrease the amount of bend in the mast by adjusting the diamonds and jumper, or we can control the degree of rotation.

Of these three variables, diamonds, jumper stay and rotation, it is the diamond stays that will require the least frequent attention. We are not suggesting for one moment that the diamond stay setting is unimportant. It certainly is. But in most cases and in most conditions the diamond stay tension can be set and left well alone for the duration of the race. In fact the Tornado rules do not permit the diamonds to be adjusted while racing.

It may require a little bit of fiddling and experimenting to determine the best setting for the diamond stays, to suit your sails and your own personal style of sailing. You will find that the best setting will have both stays slightly slack when the mast is not rotated. Once you have found the correct setting, it should only need to be altered to compensate for other changes that might have been made on the boat. For example, if a fuller sail or softer battens are used, the diamonds will need to be slackened. The reverse applies for a flatter sail or stiffer battens. The only other time the diamond stays may require alteration is for extremes in weather conditions. For both very light winds and extremely heavy winds the diamond stays should be tightened. In light winds this will prevent mast bend and keep the sail full. In very heavy winds, when the mast is set with little rotation, the diamonds will protect the mast from breakage, especially downwind.

Jumper stays are found mainly on cat-rigged boats, because they tend to foul the leech of the jib on sloop rigs. The sole purpose of the jumper stay is to limit the fore-and-aft bend in the mast. Most are fitted with a hifield lever at the lower end so that they can be released for upwind sailing to allow the mast to bend aft, and tensioned for downwind sailing pulling fullness into the sail. A further desirable refinement is to add a turnbuckle or worm screw into the system for fine adjustment.

MAKE SURE PIVOT IS NOT SLOPPY

WATER LINE

WEAR AT THIS POINT MEANS A CHANGE IN BLADE ANGLE

LEADING EDGE AT RIGHT ANGLES TO WATERLINE

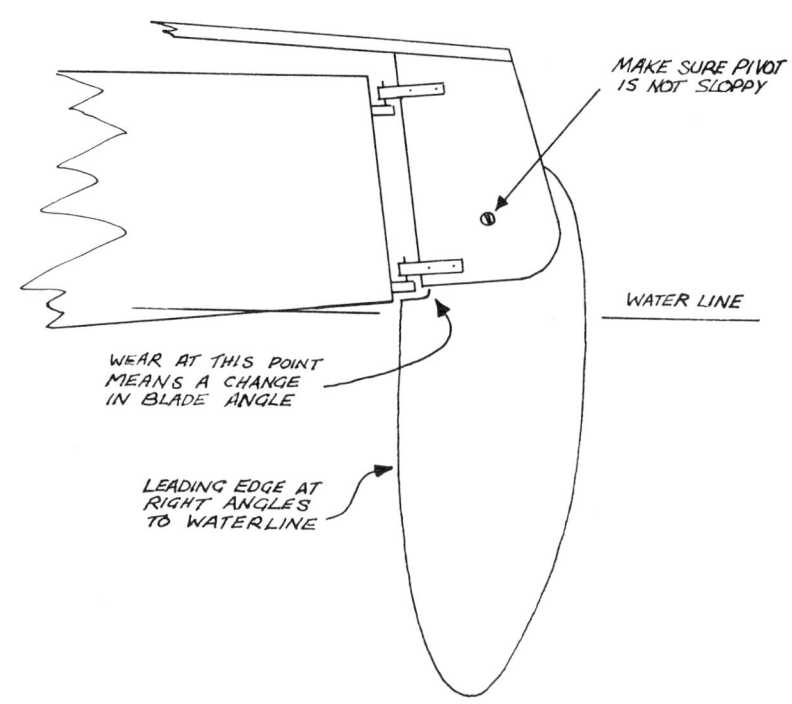

Rudder blade angle is absolutely critical to the balance of a catamaran. Any sloppiness in the fit of the blade or in the pivot point will make fine tuning of the boat almost impossible.

In other words, with the hifield lever in the 'on' position the jumper wire should be set up with more tension in light airs than it should for heavier winds.

If your class rules permit the mast to be rotated, make sure that you take advantage of this. If all the main rigging is taken from a single point at the leading edge of the mast and a low friction pivoting mast step used, the mast should be free to rotate through close to one hundred and eighty degrees. Make sure that your mast rotation control system is easy to use and preferably one that can be adjusted from the weather gunwale by either skipper or crew while the boat is being driven hard to windward. In sailing a boat to windward (and downwind, for that matter) with the mast fully rotated, it is important not to be too concerned about how the sail looks from your position on the windward gunwale. It will possibly look terrible. But remember it is the flow of the wind around the *leeward* side of the sail that provides the drive, and a fully rotated mast will considerably clean up the turbulence on the important lee side of the sail.

If we take the fore-and-aft centreline of the boat as being nought degrees and the mast when fully rotated as approximately ninety degrees let us look at the various settings of mast rotation and the effect they might have on the tuning of the rig. Most catamarans, particularly the sloop-rigged classes like the Tornado, will sail better to windward in light to moderate winds with the mast almost fully rotated.

TUNING FOR FASTER SAILING

In extremely light airs it may even be necessary to rig a system that will hold the mast in its rotated position. Certainly, in sloppy seas the mast should not be allowed to flop around on its axis.

The precise angle of mast rotation for upwind sailing will have to be found through experimentation and observation. You will be quite surprised at the marked effect a slight change in mast angle can have on the appearance of the mainsail. When you have found the angle you believe to be right, make sure that you mark your rotation control gear so that it can always be accurately set to that angle.

As the wind increases, you will notice that the centre section of the mast below the hounds will start to fall away to leeward, closing the slot between main and jib. The induced bend in the mast will also tend to hook the upper section to weather and may cause the upper leech of the sail to hook to weather also. This rather strange bending of the mast can be tolerated up to certain limits before it becomes necessary to reduce the amount of mast rotation. The clean air flow around the lee side of the mast and mainsail seems to be more important to the boat's performance than the slightly hooking leech and the main/jib slot configuration. Depending on the fullness of your sails, it is worth experimenting with the mainsheet and jib sheet travellers when the mast starts to distort in this manner. The boat will possibly sail easier with both set a little further to leeward.

As the breeze further increases and the seas start to build up, it will be necessary to reduce the amount of mast rotation. When the centre section of the mast starts surging to leeward as the boat climbs over each wave, it is time to adjust the rig to suit the conditions. It will depend on the flexibility of the spar itself, the fullness of the mainsail, and the tension on the diamonds, in what strength breeze this starts to occur. However, as a basic principle, keep the mast in its fully rotated position for as long as possible.

In order to determine the best rotation setting for fresh breezes quickly, it is essential for the mast to be adjusted while the boat is being driven hard to windward. The ideal adjustment system allows the crew to operate it while flat out on the trapeze. As the mast rotation is reduced the shape of the mainsail will noticeably change. The sail will appear to be flatter, particularly at the luff, and the leech will be freed. You will find that the boat will not sail as high into the breeze so you must quickly change your own technique to allow the boat to sail a little free and drive hard to windward. A rotation angle of about forty-five degrees is likely to be appropriate for winds in the eighteen to twenty-four miles per hour range.

For sailing to windward in very fresh conditions, say over twenty-five miles per hour, the mast rotation will require further adjustment. The ideal angle for these conditions seems to be one that allows the mast to bend only through its fore-and-aft axis. This angle can easily be found by moving the mast each way until the tension on each diamond stay appears to be equal.

Similar principles apply to the mast rotation setting for downwind sailing. Again, the basic idea is to use as much rotation as the conditions will allow. In fresh conditions when a rotation angle of, say, forty-five degrees is being used upwind, you will almost certainly be able to use full rotation downwind. In very hard conditions when the wind is gusting near thirty miles per hour and the seas increase the likelihood of the lee bow burying when on a beam reach, be a little careful of over-rotating the mast. It is in conditions like these that a mast is most likely to fail, and when a mast does break it folds forward at the spreaders due to over-rotation.

While on the subject of masts, there are a number of other items that might not have a great influence on the racing performance of the boat but nonetheless are still important.

Mainsail halyard locks are now used on most classes. A halyard lock is an essential piece of equipment and it must be strong and reliable in use. The type of lock commonly used on the Tornado is simple and suits all types of cat. A jib halyard lock is less common and we believe this is a worthwhile item on a sloop-rigged cat. Most of the effective jib halyard locks that we have seen have been homemade out of stainless steel. They are simply a small hook that is clamped to the forestay and held at a pre-determined height by a fixed length wire. The peak of the jib carries a stainless steel ring which, with a little juggling, will fall onto the hook. The jib luff is then tensioned from the bottom.

If possible you should make your mast watertight. The reason for this is obvious in that it is most helpful in the event of a capsize. And only a fool believes he will never capsize!

Finally, a word about fittings and fastenings on the mast. We have all heard and read many times of the importance of keeping gear on the upper mast down to a minimum and of having that gear as neat and tidy as possible to reduce drag. This applies just as much on a catamaran, perhaps even more because of the higher apparent wind speeds. 'Pop'-type rivets in monel metal of three-sixteenths of an inch diameter are adequate for fastening most items to the mast, although it is wise to use bolts enclosed in tube for the hounds fitting, main shrouds and forestay. On a sloop rig, it is most important to keep all fittings at the base of the mast, including the mast rotation lever, as neat as possible to avoid fouling of the jib sheets when tacking.

THE BOOM

Over the years the function of the boom has changed. Once the boom's main purpose was to contain the foot of the sail. Today, however, the boom is simply a prop to keep the clew of the sail out from the mast, plus a very handy place to attach the sundry sail adjusting gear.

The boom attaches to the mast at the gooseneck and there are two different types of fitting used. The gooseneck is either sliding or fixed. If it is of the sliding type, it runs on a track on the back of the mast (or in the sail track) and moves down when the luff of the sail is tensioned. A fixed gooseneck remains in the one position on the mast and the sail luff downhaul is an independent fitting. Although the trend on the high performance classes is towards a fixed boom, it is not a significant factor in the tuning of the boat, provided, of course, that the mainsail luff can be tensioned easily while racing.

The mainsail luff tension is a most critical factor in the performance of a racing cat and an adjustment system must be used, enabling this to be changed from either side of the mast while the boat is sailing to windward. On some classes, this downhaul system can be led along the boom for easy crew access.

At the outer end of the boom is the clew outhaul. These are now standard on most cats and are very similar in their design and function. Basically, they allow the clew of the mainsail to be adjusted while the boat is sailing, thus increasing or decreasing the fullness of the lower part of the sail.

The boom will also carry the leech line

TUNING FOR FASTER SAILING 115

Max Press sails an early model Australis. This particular boat is very simply rigged but the essentials are there: clew outhaul, boom vang-cum-mast rotation control, luff downhaul and full width hawse. More fancy items missing include leech line, trapeze height adjusters, rigging hifield and centrepoint uphaul.

adjustment system whether this is for an internal leech cord or an external wire leech line.

The adjustment of the leech line and the clew outhaul are both critical to the tuning of a racing cat whether it be a cat rigged mono-type or a two-man sloop.

By far the most effective form of leech line is the external variety that leads through the ends of the battens to the headboard on the sail. It is most important that the guides for the wire on the ends of the battens run very freely and that they prescribe a 'fair curve' when the sail is hoisted. This will ensure that the 'push' exerted by the leech line on each batten towards the mast will be even.

A leech line will rarely be required when sailing upwind. Perhaps in very light airs some tension on the leech line may help in pulling artificial fullness into an otherwise flat sail. Or if you have set up the boat for heavy winds and have fitted stiff battens, a leech line may help compensate should the breeze fade.

If you are racing with the leech line on in light winds you will find that it tends to hook the leech of the sail to windward. This will increase the weather helm of the boat, so the mainsheet traveller should be eased to leeward to compensate.

An adjustable leech line will really pay off when sailing downwind. On any leg of the course broader than a lead, some tension on the wire leech line will increase the drive and power of the mainsail. The amount of tension required on the leech line will depend on a number of variable factors including sail fullness, batten stiffness, wind strength, and sea conditions. The leech line should be pulled on hard enough to increase the fullness of the sail, particularly the upper one-third, yet not so hard that it starts to hook the leech to windward.

The clew outhaul is another form of sail adjustment that will require constant attention throughout a race. With the clew adjuster hauled on — that is, away from the mast — the lower part of the sail is flattened. With it released, the shock cord will pull the clew forward, pushing fullness into the sill batten and the lower part of the sail.

In fact, it is true to say that on most rigs the position of the clew outhaul will influence the shape of the *entire* sail and not just the lower part. Although it will not affect the actual fullness of the upper sail, it does have some influence over the shape because the position of the downward load on the leech is affected when the clew outhaul is moved.

For upwind sailing in most conditions, the clew outhaul should be in the 'on' position with the sill batten pulled very nearly straight. In light airs it can be eased slightly to add fullness to the sail. But if eased too much, the lower part of the sail will distort badly. The clew is allowed to move forward for downwind sailing, combining with the leech line to increase the drive of the sail.

On most small racing dinghies, and even on some of the ocean racers, some form of boom downhaul is used for downwind sailing. The boom vang is the most common means used to strap the boom down but a vang is not always easy to rig on a catamaran. If the gooseneck is close to the mast step and the boom angles upward, an effective boom vang of the conventional type is almost impossible to rig. The loads exerted on the boom, the gooseneck, the mast and the vang itself are very high on a catamaran and often the boom vang is the cause of otherwise unnecessary breakages.

There are two widely accepted alternatives to the boom vang for the racing catamaran. The first is the transverse mainsheet traveller or hawse. With the very strong and light free-running track that is now readily available, it is possible to run the mainsheet hawse right across the full width of the boat. For most downwind sailing conditions, the mainsheet traveller can be adjusted to enable the mainsheet to provide the downhaul effect usually left to the boom vang.

A second alternative to the boom vang is a piece of gear commonly referred to as a 'go fast'. This is a rope that leads from about halfway along the boom down

TUNING FOR FASTER SAILING

through a fairlead at the gunwale a couple of feet aft of the chainplate, and then across the boat to a cleat handy to the skipper or crew. When the boat comes off the wind the mainsheet is freed and the 'go fast' hauled on and cleated. The mainsheet is then hauled in again and the combination of the load on the 'go fast' and the mainsheet has the effect of pulling the boom down hard. This 'go fast' can easily be set up as an endless rope that leads from the boom, down through a fairlead at the gunwale, across the boat and through another fairlead at the opposite gunwale, and up to the boom once more. It is a most effective piece of equipment but does tend to get in the way when tacking.

Whether you are able to rig an effective boom vang on your cat or you use a full width hawse, and maybe a 'go fast', is not critical, but some form of boom downhaul for downwind sailing is essential. The relatively high aspect ratio rig on most catamarans will very readily develop twist unless strapped down. And a twisting mainsail is very bad news when off the wind.

SAILS AND BATTENS

It would be a simple matter for us to say that to win races you must have the best sails and battens that are the right shape. So at the risk of seeming to take the easy route we will say it anyhow!

Old sails rarely perform well, and soft or spongy misshapen battens can very quickly spoil the best sail. Assuming that you have recently purchased a new sail or sails for your boat, where should you start in making sure that you get the best out of them?

Most catamaran mainsails carry through-battens, as many as ten or twelve to a sail, and nowadays most catamaran jibs carry small leech battens.

This is Quest II *winning a Little America's Cup heat off Thorpe Bay in 1965. The jib/mainsail slot appears to be nearly perfect for these light conditions.*

The materials available for sail battens vary considerably depending on what part of the world you happen to sail in. For many years cane was considered the ideal material in that it had great flexibility and springyness, and was light and relatively easy to work into shape. Today cane is rarely used for cat sail battens. The supply of high quality cane seems to have dried up and what we buy today as batten cane is often of very poor quality. Also, cane battens do tend to lose their spring after a time and must be replaced or re-shaped.

Various types of hardwood can be used and may be quite suitable. We have seen excellent sail battens made from Ramin, Oak, Ash, Hickory and Sugar Pine. It is not so much the type of timber that is used but the quality of the actual piece that is important. Most straight-grained, air-dried hardwoods are suitable for sail battens, but all of these will tend to lose their springyness with age. To delay this, the battens should be painted or varnished to prevent moisture penetration, and they should never be rolled up in a wet sail or left lying in the hot sun.

Of all the batten materials available, fibreglass or fibreglass reinforced hardwood seem to be the most suitable and most reliable. With a fibreglass batten it is a little more difficult to get the initial shape just right, but once shaped, the batten will conform to this shape for all time.

In most areas where cats are sailed, professionally manufactured battens are available. But a word of caution here. While the quality of manufacture of these battens might be quite satisfactory, the actual shape might be suspect. So make sure that if you do purchase a professional batten, it is of the type that allows you to do your own fiddling at home.

There is no such thing as the perfect shape for a sail batten that applies to all battens for all sails for all sailing conditions. There are, however, some basic requirements for a batten shape which must be followed.

The location of the 'drive' in the batten is important. By 'drive' we mean the point of maximum curve. As a general rule the drive is further forward on a cat-rigged mainsail than one on a sloop rig. The drive in the battens for a bendy rig will also be further forward than for a stiff rig. This is because the bending of the mast has the effect of moving the drive aft in the sail.

The leech end of a batten must be firm and straight, particularly the final third of its length. One function of a sail batten on a catamaran is to minimize the hooking leech when the leech line is on, or when the mast is fully rotated. And, perhaps most important of all, the position of the drive in the battens must be consistent throughout the sail from peak to foot. Because the mainsheeting systems used on most cats exert tremendous pressures on the leech of the sail, the one or two top battens in the sail should always be relatively heavier than the battens lower in the sail.

The primary function of a mainsail batten is to *hold* the shape in the sail and not to give the sail a shape other than that put there by the sail maker. Battens can vary in stiffness to suit different wind strengths, but if a sail has more than one set of battens, each set should have basically the same shape.

There are various ways of measuring the comparative deflection of battens, perhaps the most common being to measure with a small spring balance the load required to deflect the batten. This is fine if you are sorting through a large bundle of battens and wish to grade them in order of stiffness, but it can never replace the best method of measurement — trying them in the sail.

Jib leech battens are much more simple. They are quite necessary for the long-term correct setting of a jib but they are there for the sole purpose of preventing leech curl and the flutter that would result. Jib battens can be made of practically any material that will remain straight in the sail but has sufficient 'give' to prevent breakages. Small pieces of cane, or even thin, flat pieces of plastic, are quite satisfactory.

A final point about sail battens, and one that we feel quite strongly about, is that in tuning a catamaran, it should be a primary objective ultimately to have the boat sailing well in all conditions without the need to change battens. Once on the course, you can never change your sail battens. You are stuck with them for the

TUNING FOR FASTER SAILING

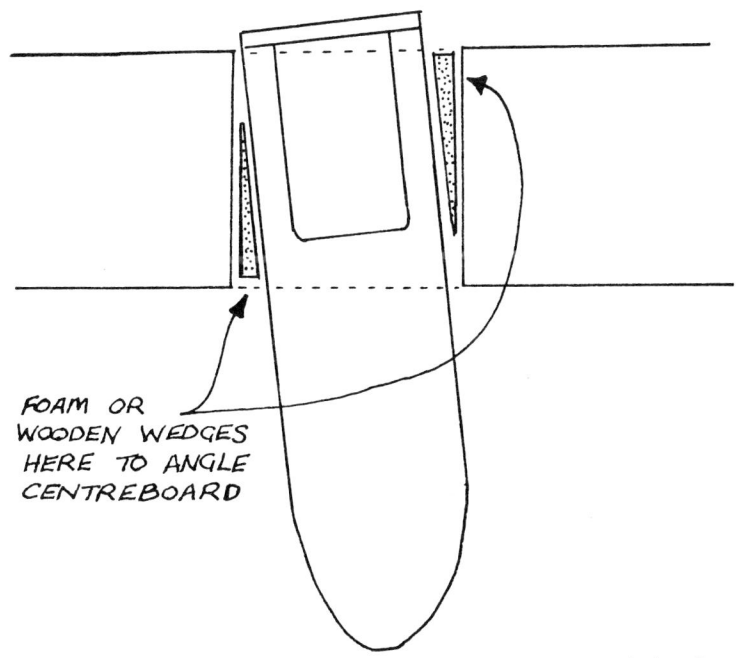

FOAM OR WOODEN WEDGES HERE TO ANGLE CENTREBOARD

If the centreboard case is long enough the board can be angled using foam or wooden wedges in the positions shown.

entire race so ideally you should try always to be in the position where you have the right set in the sail. You will only achieve this if you use only one set of battens for all conditions, and rely on the other adjustable gear on the boat to cope with any desired changes in sail shape.

We have already discussed much of the adjustable gear required on a racing catamaran to modify sail shape during a race, to take advantage of the conditions or to sail efficiently on each leg of the course. The basic principles of sail trimming that apply for all sailing boats are equally applicable to catamarans. It is in the very fine degrees of adjustment that the differences occur.

On a mainsail there are four main variables which must all be working together to get the boat sailing at its best to windward. These are:
  Luff tension.
  Mast rotation.
  Clew outhaul.
  Mainsheet traveller.

In heavy winds it can be generally stated that you should increase luff tension, use less mast rotation, haul on the clew outhaul, and ease the traveller anything from six to eighteen inches off centre. The procedure is reversed for light airs.

On a jib there are three variables which require attention:
  Luff tension.
  Sheeting position, fore and aft.
  Sheeting position, in and out.

Heavier winds require a tighter luff, and an open slot between main and jib. Hence the sheeting position should be moved aft and outboard. Like the main, the procedure is reversed for lighter winds.

Those are the basic principles. The

precise positions will be determined with practice and experience. Remember to have some form of calibration on all the adjustable gear to aid your memory.

Experimentation, trial and error, must be continued if you are to get the best out of your boat in keen racing. But all this will be wasted unless there is some method in your experimenting. It is absolutely pointless unless you are racing or have a trial horse handy to measure against. It is also important to make only one alteration at a time and to do this when all the other factors, wind, sea condition and so on, remain unaltered.

As a guide to your cat tuning we have set out below some of the more common problems together with a number of suggestions as to their cause.

Lee helm
Rudder blades angled forward of right-angles to waterline.
Jib leech too tight.
Mast raked too far forward.
Centreboards angled too far aft.
Mainsail leech slack or stretched.
Mainsheet traveller too far to leeward.
Crew weight too far aft.
Full jib, flat mainsail.

Weather helm
Rudder blades angled aft.
Jib lacking drive or sheeted too far aft or too far to leeward.
Centreboard vertical or angled forward.
Mast raked aft.
Mainsail too full with hooking leech (a common cause).
Mainsheet traveller too central.
Crew weight too far forward.
Full mainsail, flat jib.
Mast too stiff in fresh winds.

Boat readily flies a hull but will not drive
Mast over-rotated.
Mainsail leech too tight or hooking. (Leech line still on!)
Traveller too central.
Mast too stiff.
Drive in sails too far aft.
Mast raked too far forward.

Boat lacks power to windward
Sails too flat.
Battens too stiff or have lost their spring.
Mast too flexible.
Old sails that have lost their stability.
Boat is heavy.
Mainsail/jib slot not working.
Sheets in too hard.

Boat will not point to windward
Jib sheeted too far forward.
Drive in mainsail too far aft.
Poor centreboard and rudder shape.
Twist in mainsail.
Main/jib slot closed.
Skipper trying to 'pinch'.

Poor downwind performance
Too much luff tension on main and jib.
Mast raked aft.
Rudder blade angle incorrect.
Mainsail allowed to develop twist.
Jib sheeted too close to main.
Leech line is hooking leech rather than increasing sail drive.
Crew weight too far aft.
Mast not fully rotated.
Mast allowed to flop around pivot point.

Gear, Gadgets and Sundry Hardware

8

One of the pleasures associated with the racing of a sailing boat is the many hours that can be spent tinkering with or thinking about the gear. When it comes to designing or modifying a fitting, we all pretend that we are amateur inventors and we get quite a kick out of solving a particular technical problem. Many a pleasant lunch hour can also be wiled away, browsing through the displays at your local ship's chandlery.

Only a few years ago, considerable

This superbly well prepared Tornado has a number of interesting features in the gear and gadget department. The following items are of special interest:
  a. Feather wind indicator mounted forward of jib tack.
  b. Bridgedeck has fore-and-aft central beam which provides additional fitting attachment points.
  c. Last two blocks on mainsheet are ratchets.
  d. Tillers are long with crossbar forward of sheet.
  e. Tiller extensions extend from tillers enabling skipper to steer with his foot, as he is here.
  f. Gunwale has foot loops forward for choppy seas and foot loops aft for reaching.
  g. Jib sheet system has wire leads from clew to reduce sheet length and windage.
  h. Leech line adjuster has single purchase.
  i. Flat side of box section boom is ideal place for writing course.

improvisation was necessary when setting up the gear on a catamaran. Nowadays, the range of small boat fittings and equipment is vastly improved and many of the fitting manufacturers produce specially designed catamaran items. The quality and the range of 'off the shelf' fittings available from the leading makers is of an excellent standard and, even better, they are usually marketed throughout the world to cater for the internationalism of yacht racing.

But, of course, it is one thing to have available a large range of high quality (and, incidentally, high priced) gear but this does not help the boat owner to choose the *right* gear when setting up his boat. If you are a relative newcomer to catamaran racing or are new to a particular class, we would suggest that you take a very close look at the leading boats in the fleet. The best boat will not always have the best arrangement of gear, but by looking at the top two or three boats, you can be reasonably sure of being on the right track. If you can, take some photographs of these boats, and ask their owners' advice. If you have a crew, take him along too when you study the leading boats and try and work out your gear together.

Another very useful source of information on fittings and gear is a Boat Show. Many countries in the world have an annual boat show, especially those where yacht racing is one of the more popular sports. They are usually held in midwinter, and provide an ideal opportunity to study the leading boats of a number of different classes. How much you ultimately change from the layout of the leading boats when setting up your own will depend to a large degree on the depth of your own racing experience. As a general rule it will pay to adopt a 'follow the leader' approach if your experience is limited.

Most yachtsmen seem to be highly individualistic in that simply copying the gear on the leading boats in the fleet rarely keeps them happy for long. They will usually be looking for improvement, or what they believe to be improvement anyway, and making changes to the gear or modifying it in one way or another. Although we have said that there is a vast range of standard gear available, most boat owners will enjoy making up their own bits and pieces to improve the efficiency of their boat.

A fully equipped engineering machine shop is not required if you are to make simple fittings, but a few tools — all readily available — will be necessary. We would suggest that you start with the following items:

Bench vice.
Hammer.
Screwdriver — large and small.
Adjustable spanner.
Pliers.
File — flat and round.
Centrepunch.
High-speed drills.
Hand or power drill.
Hacksaw — high-speed blades, 32 teeth to inch.

Plus an assortment of stainless steel bolts, nuts, washers, split pins and rivets.

These are the basic items but it is also handy to have some scraps of stainless steel plate (16 and 12 gauge), aluminium plate, aluminium tube (3/8" and 1/2"), stainless steel wire and stainless steel rod. Scraps such as these can often be picked up for next to nothing from a sheet metal fabricator.

If you find that you have a flair for making fittings and creating gadgets for the boat, a few more advanced tools will be needed. These include:

'Pop'-type riveter.
Swage tool.

GEAR, GADGETS AND SUNDRY HARDWARE

A simple boat with simple gear. On this Australian designed 14' Arrow, sail and mast control equipment has been kept to a minimum. This boat later won two national titles with very little modification. Intermediate stays were removed from the mast and forward diamond stays added. Also a parallel inner track was added for the jib sheet fairlead slide.

Thread cutting taps and dies.

Gas welding equipment.

These more elaborate items can be quite expensive and will be beyond the means of many average home catamaran builders. One suggestion, which in our experience can work extremely well, is to pool your resources with a few of your sailing friends. For example, you might buy a swage tool, swages and ferrules, while one of your friends buys a riveter and rivets. It then is a simple matter to borrow the necessary tools as required.

Assuming that you are nearing completion of a new boat or have just taken delivery of a new boat from a builder, you must now decide just what gear you need to fit out the boat. Many classes include a fitting list in their building instructions, and this can be used as a guide. Unfortunately, this fitting list rarely keeps pace with the trends in fittings in the class, so do not be afraid to vary from this. To select the fittings, sit down with a large sheet of paper, the plans of your boat, photographs, magazine articles or other reference material for the particular class, plus two or three fitting manufacturer's catalogues. If your local fitting shop will not give you the catalogues, they will certainly let you take them home to study over a weekend.

You should make a rough sketch of the boat, and then go through all the essential systems that will be required, together with the fittings that make up each system. Initially, only worry about the essential systems. Then, on Monday morning, head for the ship's chandler with your list of bits plus about twice the amount of money that you had originally budgeted for. Do not worry about ordering all the fittings required because the retailer will certainly exchange any that you later find to be unsuitable — provided of course that you have not been sailing. Once the boat is set up with all the essential gear, you can consider the 'fancy' stuff. In fact, we would suggest that you take your boat sailing a few times before you finalize your plans for the more elaborate gear.

All the fittings and gear on a racing catamaran can generally be classified into three separate categories. Sometimes, of course, these categories overlap, but basically they are:
1. *Structural* — beam bolts and clamps, beams, dolphin striker, chain-plates, etc.
2. *Fixed, or non-adjustable* — hiking straps, trampoline, rudder gudgeons, centreboard pivots, most standing rigging, spreaders, boom, mast, halyards and sheaves, halyard lock, etc.
3. *Adjustable* — all sheets, mainsheet hawse, leech line, boom vang, sail luff downhaul, clew outhaul, centreboard uphaul, etc.

Many of the fittings and gadgets that can be used or that can be built have been mentioned in earlier chapters, but these few further hints might be helpful when fitting out your boat or when making improvements.

In the area of *structural* fittings it is usually wise to follow the plans rather than attempting to improvise. The dolphin striker, beam bolts and clamps must be very strong and little weight can be saved by using lighter material than that specified. The only suggestion that we do make is to look for ways of making the boat more easy to assemble and dismantle. For example, if the beam clamps are not all identical, number them from one to eight, starting at the port outside clamp on the main beam and ending at the starboard outside clamp on the aft beam. The numbers can easily be permanently marked on the underside of the clamps using a centrepunch.

It is in the other two categories of fittings that there is the most opportunity for using your own ideas or for adapting standard gear to suit your own purposes.

Hiking straps. Basically, there are two different types; those that are sewn to the trampoline and those that stretch fore and aft across the trampoline, being fastened to the main and aft beam. With either type the webbing must be strong, without stretch and at least two, preferably three inches wide. If the straps are sewn to the trampoline, make sure that there is sufficient slackness in the strap to take your feet comfortably. Too much slackness, however, will be most uncomfortable and allow your feet to lift too high when hiking out.

Small foam pads placed between the trampoline and the hiking strap will keep the strap slightly raised and make it easier to get your feet underneath in a crisis. In order to provide added leverage for the crew when moving around the trampoline, especially when hiking, some boats use long pieces of plastic tube contained in pockets running fore-and-aft along the trampoline just inboard of the hiking straps.

One of the advantages of the hiking strap that runs from the main beam to the aft beam is that the tension is more easily

GEAR, GADGETS AND SUNDRY HARDWARE 125

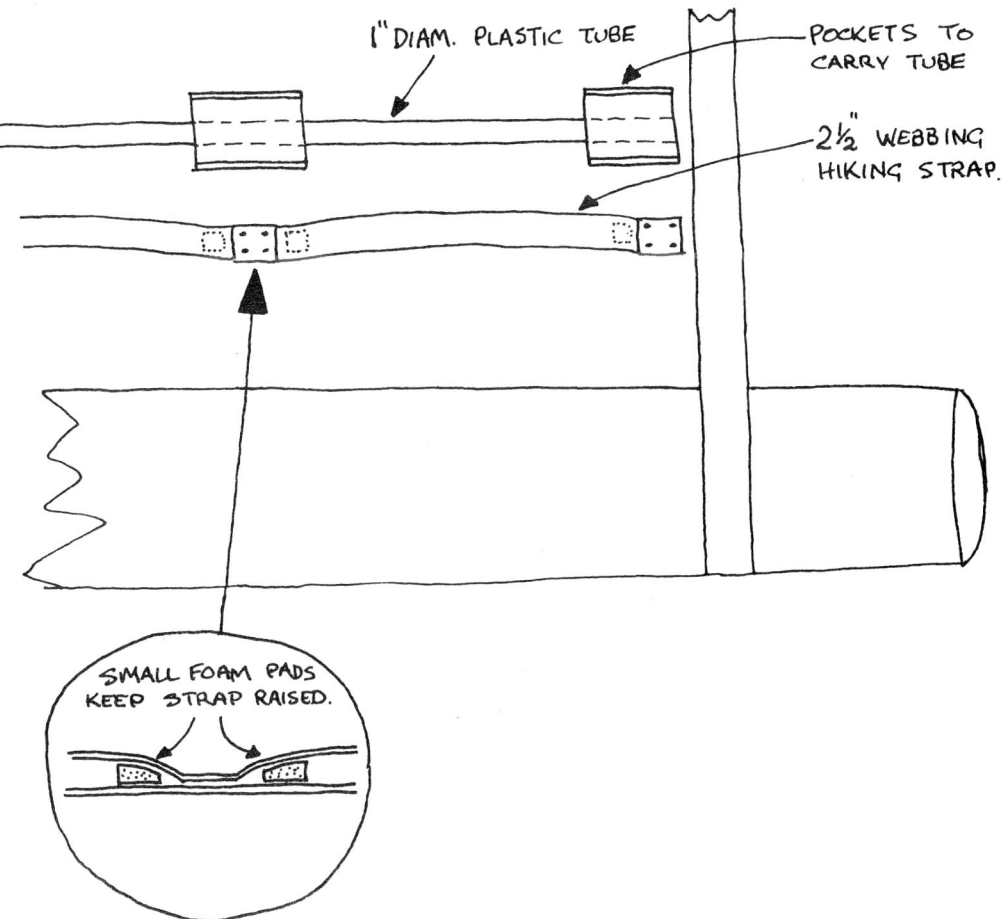

Small pieces of foam, about 2" thick, glued under the hiking strap will keep the strap clear of the trampoline. The plastic tube along the trampoline will provide both of the crew with extra foothold and will not add much weight to the boat.

adjusted. Also, the strap is constantly clear of the trampoline for quick use. Wire or heavy rope can be used as an alternative to webbing with this system, provided, of course, that it is suitably covered and will not cut into your feet when in use. Heavy plastic tube or garden hose is a suitable covering.

Trampoline. These vary, of course, from class to class but they have a number of common features. All trampolines are inclined to fill with water when racing in rough seas. The weight of this water can be considerable and will retard the boat until it drains away. All trampolines, therefore, should have adequate drain holes, and sections cut away to leeward and aft to clear the water quickly.

All trampolines have some facility for lacing them tight, whether this be down the centre, along the ends, or along the

The fore-and-aft beam under this trampoline has been extensively drilled to try and save weight.

inwales. The tension on the trampoline should always be kept quite firm, so the lacing should be non-stretch and set up so that it can easily be re-tensioned between races.

Most trampolines are fitted with a pocket or two for the stowing of gear and halyard tails. These pockets are best kept towards the forward end of the trampoline with the opening facing forward. There should be one or two press studs on the opening to keep it closed when racing.

Unfortunately, the heavy sail cloth used in most trampolines is affected by sunlight. If the boat is left for long periods with the trampoline attached and without a cover, the stitching will break down first, then eventually the cloth itself will lose its strength and fail. If you are forced to leave your boat for long periods in the open, either remove the trampoline or invest in a boat cover. A boat cover will save you money in the long run and it also provides some security for gear left on the boat.

Rudder gudgeons. When these are bolted onto transom sterns, they always seem to work loose. The bottom gudgeon, particularly, is under continuous variable loads while sailing and unless the bolts are very firm they will move in the holes and eventually loosen. We suggest that the rudder gudgeon bolts are set in a rubberized caulking compound, that very large washers are used inside the transoms and that spring washers are used under the nuts.

The gudgeons should also have some

GEAR, GADGETS AND SUNDRY HARDWARE 127

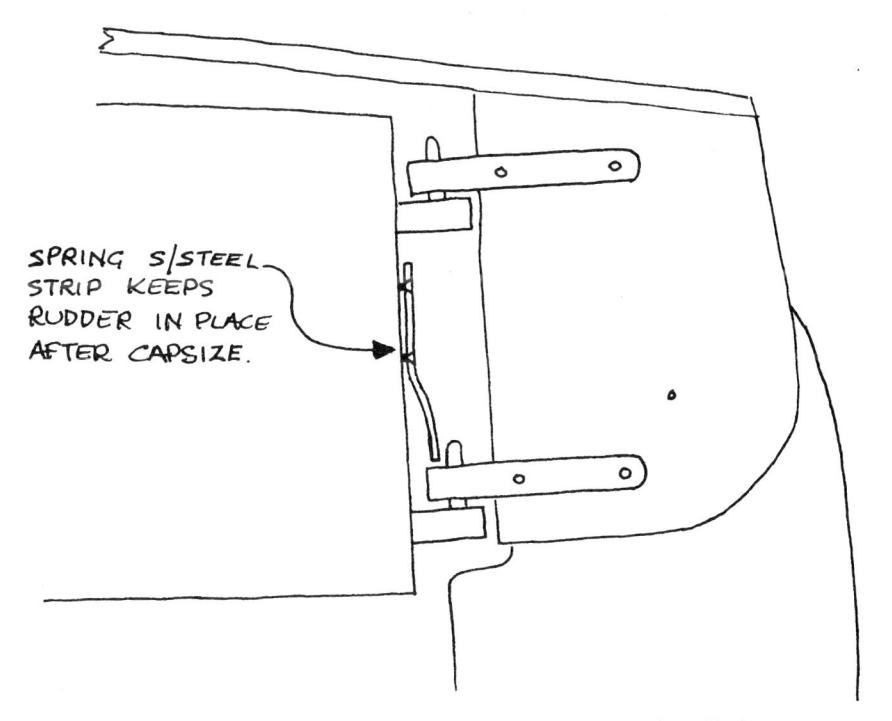

SPRING S/STEEL STRIP KEEPS RUDDER IN PLACE AFTER CAPSIZE.

When catamarans capsize, they often turn upside down and this is likely to cause one or both of the rudders to fall off. Here is one simple method of preventing this happening.

sort of a device to prevent the rudder from falling off in the event of a capsize. This requirement has been written into the Tornado class rules.

Centreboard pivots. There are two main points to watch with these. Firstly, that they are easy to remove, which in turn makes the centreboard easy to remove and replace. It is most important for top racing performance that the edges and the finish of the centreboards are kept in perfect condition and their easy removal will facilitate this.

The centreboard pivot bolt or pin should be of fairly large diameter – at least half an inch. Although a smaller diameter pivot might be quite strong enough, it will tend to enlarge the hole in the boards and make the board sloppy in the case.

Standing rigging. To say that the standing rigging is important is to rather state the obvious. Yet often the standing rigging is not given the attention it warrants and failure results. Unfortunately, a failure of the standing rigging usually results in other serious damage. We would advise that all the main standing rigging attachment points be bolted through the mast. It is true that the 'Pop' type of rivets are quite strong enough to withstand normal loads but as the mast fittings are often subjected to unusual loads, the fittings can tend to work loose after a period of use.

In order to keep drag to a minimum, all fittings on the mast must be as neat as possible. This applies particularly to the gear aloft that carries the standing rigging. Cut all bolts flush with the nuts and make sure that all metal tangs sit flush against the mast. Whether or not you can use the internal attachment method for main shrouds and diamond stays will depend on the mast section being used and if the mast is fixed or rotating.

right: Quest III's *standing rigging was solid stainless steel of aerofoil section. Each of the four stays was connected, through a series of pulleys, to the mast, and always remained parallel to the mast as it rotated. This is the control drum on the bottom of one of the forestays. The double uprights on the tip of the bow support the apparent wind indicator.*

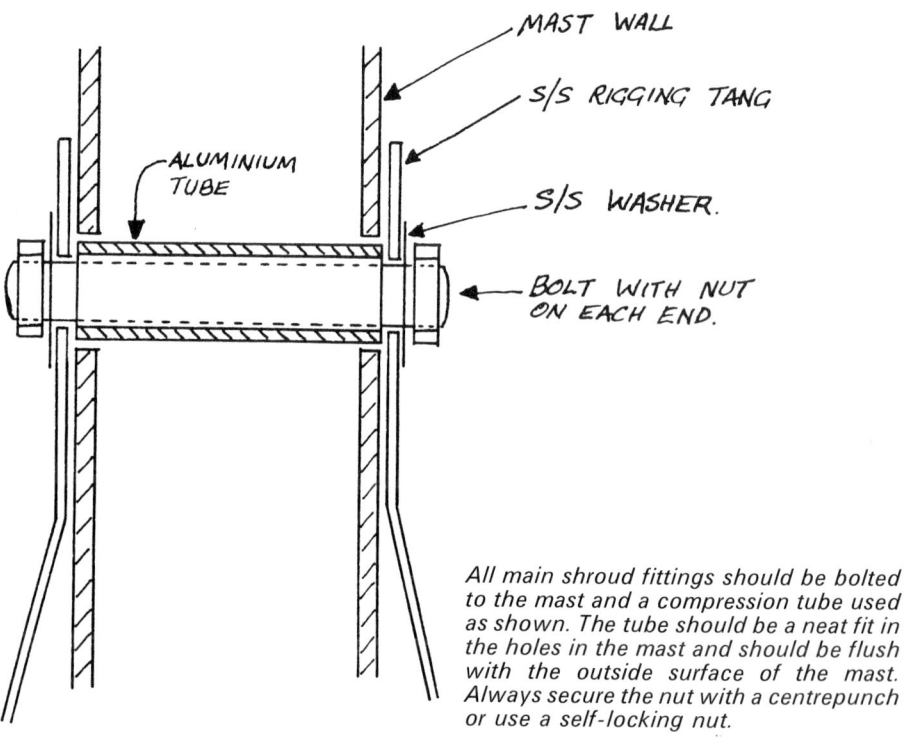

All main shroud fittings should be bolted to the mast and a compression tube used as shown. The tube should be a neat fit in the holes in the mast and should be flush with the outside surface of the mast. Always secure the nut with a centrepunch or use a self-locking nut.

GEAR, GADGETS AND SUNDRY HARDWARE

A very neat idea for adjusting diamond stays. The stainless steel box tube on the front of the mast contains a rigging screw with the bottom end fixed and the top end free to slide in the slots. The screw and adjuster pin disappears through a hole in the box tube and mast when not in use. This fitting was seen on a Tornado and worked very well. But it has now been removed to comply with class rules. However, it might prove useful on other classes.

If you are using rigging screws on the diamond stays, always make sure that they are wired so that they cannot possibly undo. No matter how tight the lock nuts are, they are still likely to work loose, particularly if they are knocked by the jib sheets on every tack.

Spreaders. Many modern cat classes now use relatively light mast sections and stiffen the mast with a set of diamond stays, and sometimes a jumper stay as well. On a mast that does not rotate, the spreaders can be quite lightly built as most of the load they will carry will be in compression.

On a rotating mast, however, the spreaders must be immensely strong to withstand the bending loads, both for-

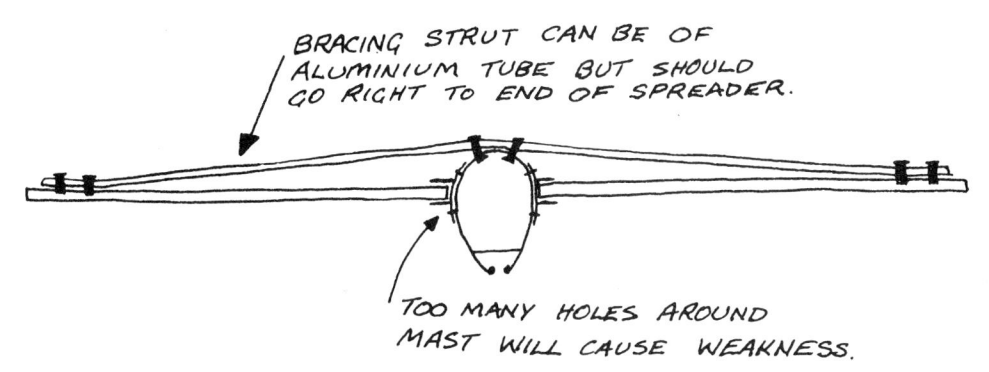

BRACING STRUT CAN BE OF ALUMINIUM TUBE BUT SHOULD GO RIGHT TO END OF SPREADER.

TOO MANY HOLES AROUND MAST WILL CAUSE WEAKNESS.

Diamond spreaders can be both light and strong. The bracing strut must go right to the ends of the spreader and be securely fastened to the front of the mast. Be careful not to drill too many holes around the mast at the spreader attachment point as this will weaken the mast.

E

ward and back. Tube, either aluminium or stainless steel, is the best material to use. Make sure that the bracing of the spreader goes right to the very end of the arm itself.

Boom. Only a few years ago the main purpose of the boom was to hold and control the foot of the sail and carry the mainsheeting blocks. With the loose-footed mainsail used on most cat classes the boom still performs these basic functions but also many more. The boom now might carry the mainsail luff downhaul, leech-line control, boom vang, and clew outhaul. Most booms are aluminium and there are a number of different sections available that are quite suitable. A rectangular section is ideal as it makes the attachment of fittings an easy matter. But a tube section, or even a light mast section, can be equally suitable.

When a boom is correctly set up it should never be under a great load, unless, of course, a boom vang is fitted. If this is the case, the gooseneck fitting will have to be very strong to take the compression loads when sailing downwind in fresh winds.

Mast. The mast is the most important single item of gear on the boat and it can safely be said that the better the mast is set up, the better will be the boat's performance.

The clew outhaul on this Tornado uses a three-to-one tackle rather than a drum winch. The wire leech line runs inside the sail, and is led through a small pulley forward of the clew when the foot is in this position. However, for downwind sailing, the clew is eased forward to bag the sill batten, and the leech line will then lead more or less straight into the small pulley.

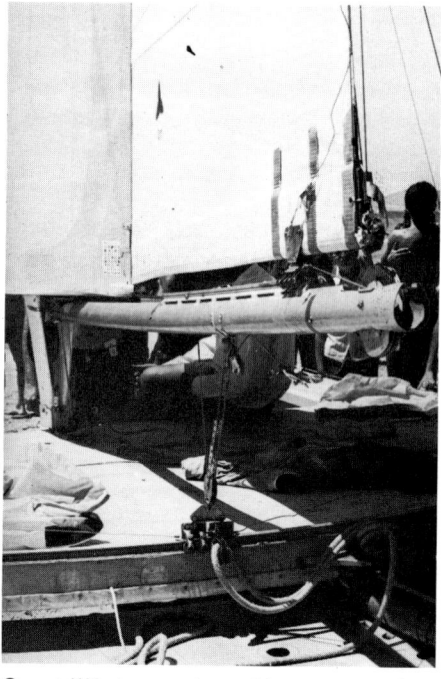

Quest III's boom viewed from astern. Sort out what all those bits and pieces do and you have much of the secret to Quest's success.

GEAR, GADGETS AND SUNDRY HARDWARE

VERY HEAVY SHOCK CORD

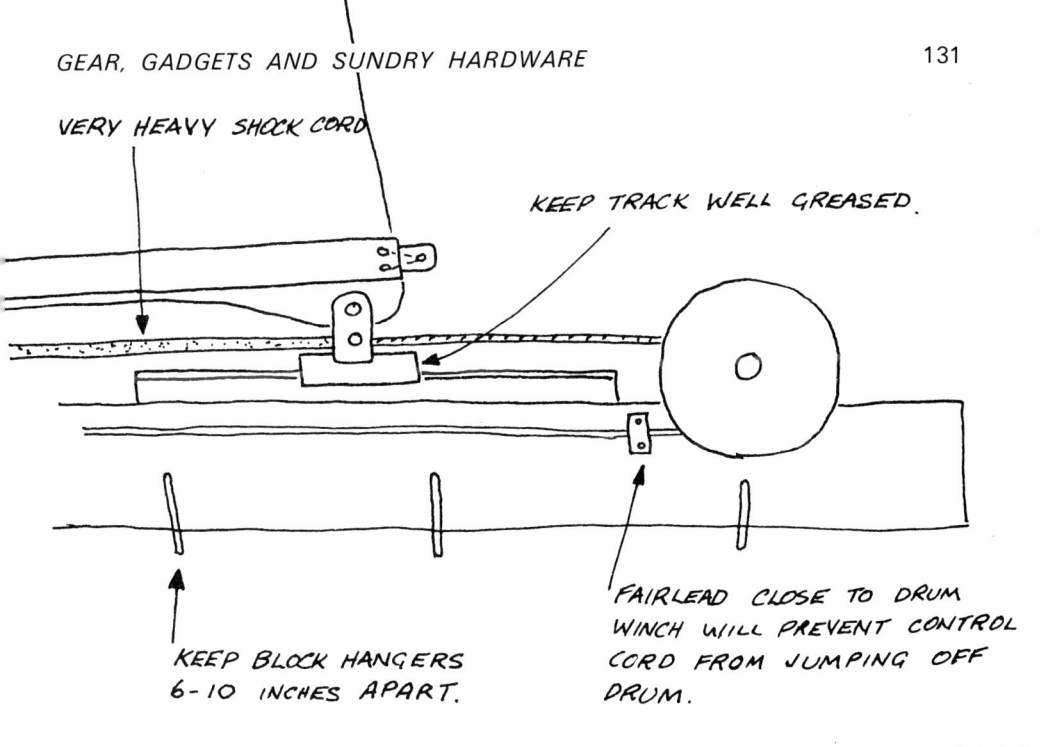

KEEP TRACK WELL GREASED.

KEEP BLOCK HANGERS 6-10 INCHES APART.

FAIRLEAD CLOSE TO DRUM WINCH WILL PREVENT CONTROL CORD FROM JUMPING OFF DRUM.

A drum winch is quite suitable for the main clew outhaul but there is always a danger of the control cord running off the drum. This can be prevented by placing the fairlead as close as possible to the drum and by using very heavy shock cord forward of the clew to keep the control line taut.

The base of Quest III's wing mast featured a heavy and very powerful winch. Quest's rig was always wound up very tight. A small trapdoor on the mast base provided access to internal control gear and was closed for racing. The mast step fitting, with hinges for raising and lowering the rig, seems incredibly light. The two angled 'legs' on the mast are made of soft wood.

We have mentioned earlier how easy it is to set up your own mast starting from a basic standard extruded length. We would advise that you do this as, apart from being a lot of fun, it does give you the opportunity of adding your own individuality to the boat. When you have finished tapering the mast length and have drilled the holes for the fittings, there are two ways you can finish the mast — by painting or anodizing. The mast can, of course, be left without any finishing and it will be quite satisfactory. However, aluminium does discolour with use and this will roughen the surface and tend to leave black stains on your sails. Anodizing is the smartest, most effective and most expensive form of finishing but not all commercial anodizers can handle

You could not find anything more simple than this mast rotation control on an Australis. The lever on the mast is at 90° when the mast is in the fore-and-aft position. The control line leads down through the hole in the beam and is adjusted from either end of the main beam using an endless loop contained within the beam.

This close-up of the mast swivelling control on Lady Helmsman *highlights the importance of having some form of calibration on all important adjustable gear.*

GEAR, GADGETS AND SUNDRY HARDWARE 133

This small piece of shaped plywood being fitted to the base of Quest III's *mast seemed to improve her upwind performance by reducing turbulence across the lower wing. The rather long boom-like pole jutting out from the base of the mast is merely part of the gear used to raise and lower the mast.*

material the length of a mast. Painting is very easy and can be quite effective. Most ship's chandlers will sell an aluminium etch primer paint and if the directions on the can are followed it will give a perfect result.

If possible, the mast should be made waterproof or as near waterproof as can be. If the whole mast cannot be sealed, the top section above the hounds should certainly be made completely watertight. The first time you experience a capsize you will be very glad that you spent time on this important task.

A boat with a mast that is easy to raise and lower will be the most enjoyable to sail. A hinged mast step is an almost essential item of equipment. With an efficient hinged mast step, it is possible for one person to step and unstep the mast on a Tornado. The mast rotation lever should be made so that it folds up as the mast is lowered, otherwise the trampoline is likely to gain an unwanted extra drain hole.

In planning the fittings on the mast of a sloop-rigged cat, try and keep the lower part of the mast as neat and as clear of protruding gear as possible. It is amazing just how easily the jib sheets will snag on even the smallest items on the mast when tacking. If you find it impossible or just impracticable to keep fittings away from the lower few feet of the mast, have your sailmaker make up a mast cover that can be laced around the lower couple of feet of the mast to prevent the sheets from getting caught.

Halyards and sheaves. Nothing is more frustrating than to have a halyard either break or jam when hoisting a sail prior to racing — and it always seems to happen when you are pressed for time.

Ideally, all halyards should be internal. Not only is this much cleaner, in that it will not interfere with the airflow around the mast, but it is also much quieter. One of the disadvantages of today's aluminium spars is the annoying metallic slap, slap, slap caused by a loose external halyard flapping in the breeze.

Any halyard that is subjected to heavy loads, even if only for short periods, should be rigged on as large a sheave as possible. A small sheave will only cause the halyard to wear prematurely and will be more inclined to seize in the sheave box.

A mainsail halyard lock is a must, and on a sloop-rigged boat a jib halyard lock is a good idea, too. The mainsail halyard lock of the type commonly seen on the Tornado is excellent and is perfected to the stage where, if correctly made, it is almost failure-proof. Jib halyard locks are still a little experimental but well worth some perseverence. If you find that a jib halyard lock cannot be rigged satisfactorily, you should consider alternative methods of keeping the jib luff tight.

Two methods are widely used. The first simply uses the forestay as the jib luff wire. The forestay is rigged and bounced down very tight from the lower end. Using a very light halyard, the jib, with zip luff, is then run up the wire and secured at the tack, and the halyard becomes the luff tensioning system. On a Tornado the rules require a light limiting wire to be contained inside the luff pocket of the sail to prevent the luff being stretched beyond the maximum dimension.

The second method, more popular on the smaller sloop-rigged cats, is for the

The simplest, most effective halyard lock of all. First seen on the IYE Tornado masts, now universally accepted on most cats.

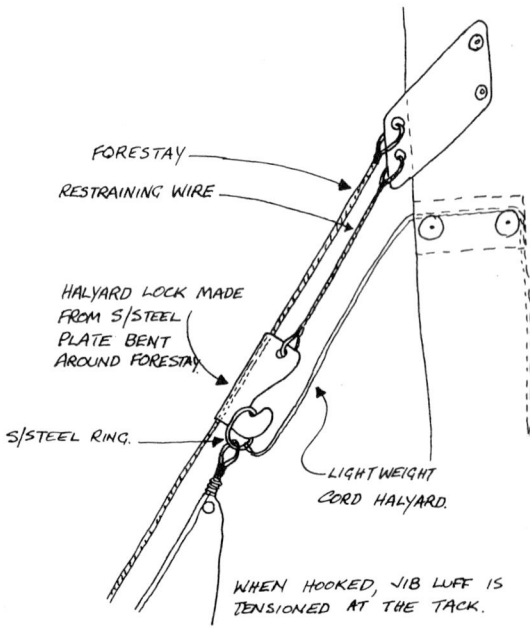

An interesting and still experimental type of jib halyard lock which is well worth trying.

GEAR, GADGETS AND SUNDRY HARDWARE

head of the jib to be shackled directly to a short wire strop leading to the hounds fitting. The rig is pulled forward and tight using the two trapeze wires, and the tack of the jib shackled to the jib bridle. Either the mast must be lowered or the boat tipped on its side to rig the jib using this method.

Mainsheet traveller. Every class seems to have its own special type of mainsheet traveller or hawse and doubtless these are all quite effective. There are, however, a few basic requirements for an efficient system that are not always taken into consideration. First, the traveller must run very freely when under the load of the sheet. Whether the hawse itself is wire, stainless steel rod, tube or the popular extruded aluminium track, it should be continually checked for wear and weaknesses. The traveller itself will be under tremendous loads in heavy winds and will need to be very strong.

There are two basic methods of controlling the position of the traveller, but of course each has its own particular variations. The traveller position can be controlled either by a single wire or rope from the centre of the boat, or by a wire or rope from each side of the boat.

The central control system has the advantage of being the most simple, but it is the more difficult to adjust while sailing the boat to windward. The dual rope system requires more rope but it can be controlled by the skipper while hard on the wind, and it has the added advantage of being able to pull the traveller to windward of the centre line, if this is required for light airs.

A popular system for controlling the mainsheet traveller. The clam cleat mounted on the aft beam is used by the skipper when sitting aft, the one mounted on the inwale is used when sitting forward. The free end of the control cord can be led to a piece of light shock-cord to keep it out of the way. The other end of the cord is tied off on a small 'd' fitting mounted about 12" to weather of the centreline. This allows the traveller to be pulled to weather in very light airs. The system is repeated on the other side of the boat.

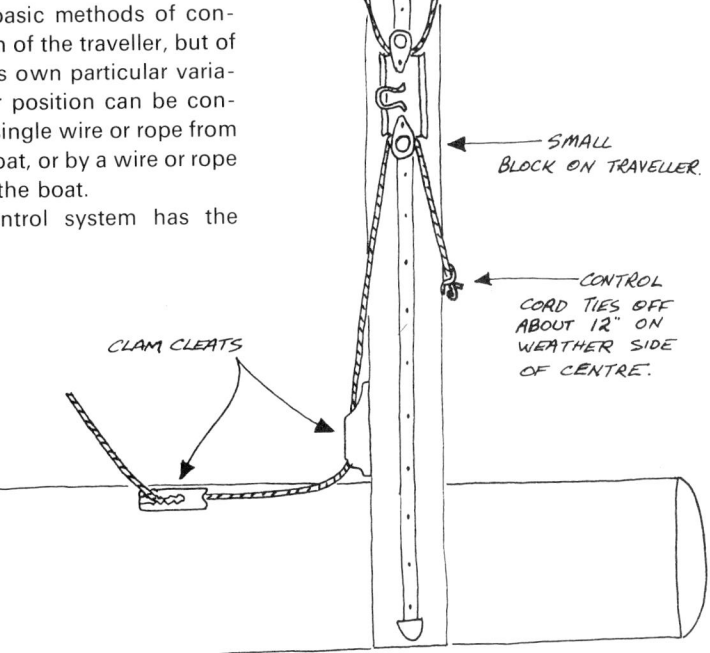

CATAMARAN SAILING TO WIN

Both these methods have the essential requirement of being self-tendering. In other words, the traveller will always return to the same pre-set position after each tack. Some of the early systems required setting after every tack but this is hopeless in highly competitive racing.

Jib sheeting position adjustment. The system illustrated is almost universally used on sloop-rigged cats. The important points to watch are that the travellers both run freely on the transverse wire, and that the control cord can be adjusted and cleated from the opposite (or weather) side of the boat while sailing hard on the wind.

Leech line. Most racing cats have a leech line of one type or another and we believe in them, especially for light weather. Many types of leech line including wire, cord and tape are enclosed in a pocket running up the leech of the mainsail. Although these might be quite effective when hauled on, there is a

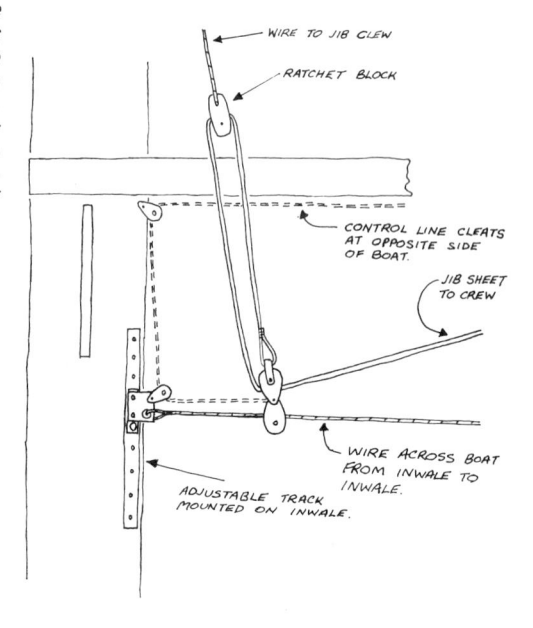

above: *Control systems need not be complicated to work effectively. This Australis has a wire hawse with simple traveller control, plus another wire to carry the final mainsheet ratchet block. The tiller extension leads under one, over the other. The clew adjuster is set on a wire rather than the heavier but more common track. Note that the free end of the mainsheet is well secured to the trampoline.*

right: *Perhaps the simplest and most effective jib sheet adjustment system. The wire running across the boat should be slack enough to allow one side to be adjusted a couple of holes forward or aft without becoming tight. A ratchet block at jib clew will be more effective than one down at deck level, because in this position the sheet turns through 180° against the notched pulley. Again, the system is repeated on the other side of the boat.*

GEAR, GADGETS AND SUNDRY HARDWARE

danger that, when eased, they will not free themselves completely, leaving the upper part of the sail to hook to windward. The external wire leech line running through plastic guides on the outer ends of the battens has proved a successful method.

For the leech line to be effective it is important that the ends of the battens prescribe a fair curve from foot to peak otherwise the leech line will exert an uneven pressure on the battens, thus causing an uneven flow in the sail.

By varying the amount of batten protruding from the leech of the sail the effect of the leech line can also be varied. For example, if your sail is rather flat in the upper section, slightly longer battens here will help overcome this when the leech line is under tension.

The leech line control is usually led along the boom to a position a couple of feet aft of the gooseneck where it can be adjusted by the crew. On a cat-rigged boat it can be led along the boom, down the mast and onto the bridgedeck for the helmsman to control. Most hifield levers will not have sufficient 'throw' for leech line control so a small three-to-one purchase with clam or cam cleat is perhaps the best method of applying the tension. For upwind sailing in fresh winds it is absolutely essential that the system allows the leech line to be completely free of tension.

Luff downhaul. The tension on the mainsail luff must be easily adjustable while racing, and of course on sloop-rigged cats the same applies for the jib luff.

A three-to-one purchase on the mainsail luff should be sufficient to pull it very tight when required, and a two-to-one advantage on the jib luff will do the job. Because the logical place to locate the main luff downhaul is on the aft edge of the base of the mast, it can sometimes be difficult for the crew to get at. This applies particularly to a rotating mast. One way to

The mainsail luff downhaul on this Australis leads through a pulley at the gooseneck and along the boom to a three-to-one tackle. This would be fairly simple for the helmsman to adjust, especially on a port tack. The leech line and clew outhaul also lead onto the boom. Different coloured cords would help identify each system. A boom vang is also fitted.

E*

overcome this is to have a fixed position gooseneck fitting, with a sheave mounted right on the top of the fitting itself. A line is then led from the tack of the sail down through the sheave and along to a control system on the top of the boom.

The cloth at the luff of the jib is not under a great load so the jib luff downhaul system can be very lightly constructed. A simple and effective method of control is to take a small diameter wire from the tack of the sail, down through a small pulley mounted at the apex of the jib bridle, down parallel with the jib bridle to the inwale, through another pulley and then back along one hull to a small purchase at the main beam.

Tillers and tiller extensions. Here there is great scope for the development of individual tastes — essentially, the best tiller and tiller extension system is the one most suited to the helmsman. An effective tiller extension will always be one that is readily accessible when required but can be stowed out of the way when not wanted. It will also be very positive in the way that it controls the rudders. There will be no slackness in the pivots and the extension will not bend when the skipper wants to round up in a hurry. The extension should only need the minimum of readying after each tack especially in strong winds.

As an added plus, the perfect tiller extension will also allow the skipper to steer the boat for short periods with something other than his hand. Whether a foot is used on the tiller, or the extension is tucked under the skipper's arm (or even under his bottom), it will facilitate rapid trimming of the boat if this can be accomplished. There will be many moments in fresh winds when a helmsman will want to adjust the mainsheet traveller while tending to the mainsheet. This becomes much easier if he can steer the boat with his foot, leaving both hands free.

One stern of Quest III. *Twin wires leading along the top of the tiller come from the rudder blade which is raised and lowered using a small winch with a crank handle. Note, too, the retaining wire with handle for the crew's use downwind.*

GEAR, GADGETS AND SUNDRY HARDWARE

A very simple and effective tiller extension set up on a Tornado. In the position shown above, the handle of the extension acts as a perfect tiller for reaching. In the position below, the skipper can move forward for upwind sailing.

140   CATAMARAN SAILING TO WIN

GEAR, GADGETS AND SUNDRY HARDWARE 141

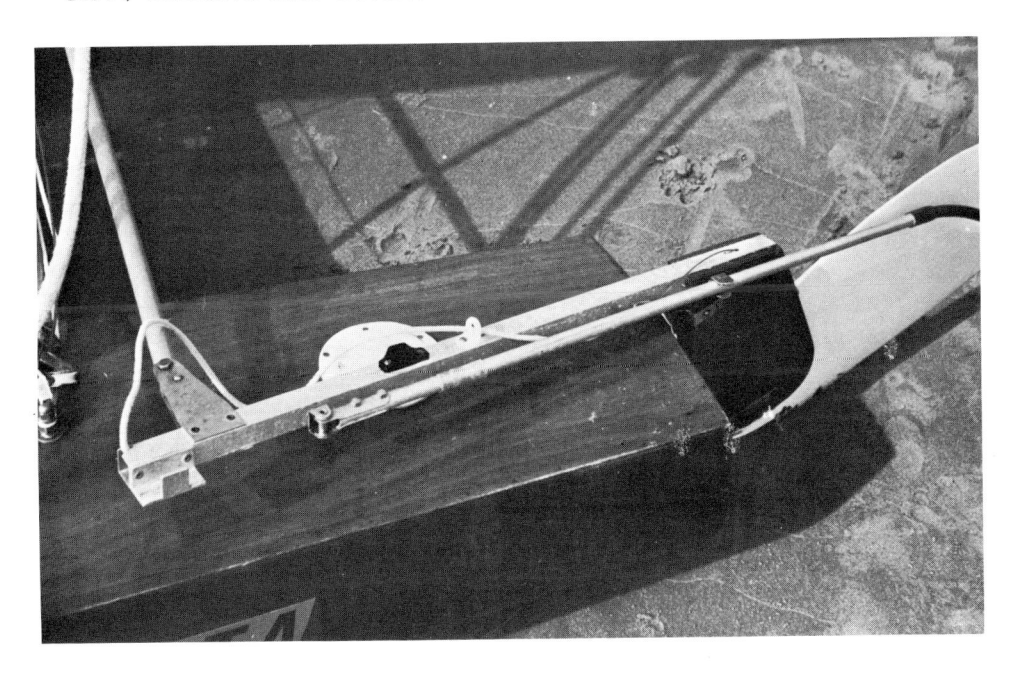

A natty three-position tiller extension seen on a Stingray class. Top left: *Extension locked in forward position allowing skipper to move well forward for light weather downwind sailing.* Bottom left: *Extension in normal upwind position. Skipper also uses trapeze on this class.* Above: *Extension locked away alongside tiller when not in use.*

Wind indicator. Here is a real opportunity for some creativity. We have seen all sorts of weird and wonderful types of wind indicator, some home made, some commercially available and others a combination of both.

A good racing skipper will always be able to sense or feel every little wind shift and would have little need for a wind indicator when sailing upwind, except in the lightest of fluky conditions. Downwind, however, is another matter. When racing a cat downwind, two factors are absolutely critical to the boat's performance. The first is the setting of the sails, and the second is the angle you are sailing at in relation to the apparent wind. An efficient, easily visible wind indicator is essential for fast downwind racing.

Many skippers prefer to have their wind indicator mounted as a mast head fly. It is true that the wind is least disturbed at the mast head but, as we have said, with the modern high aspect ratio rigs on boats such as the Tornado or International C-class, the indicator can be extremely difficult to read in this position. A more popular location is on a lightweight strut forward of the tack of the jib, at the apex of the forestay bridle.

An efficient wind indicator is of paramount importance on a racing cat. This assortment would seem to indicate that there is nothing really suitable available through your local ship's chandler, and that some improvisation is required.

top: *This is mounted forward of the top of the forestay bridle on Maurie Davies' Tornado. Maurie made the vane from a venetian blind slat.*

centre: *Peter Blaxland prefers a feather on his Tornado, mounted well forward of the disturbed air at the sail luff.*

bottom: *Another Tornado and another version of the feather.*

GEAR, GADGETS AND SUNDRY HARDWARE 143

right: *This is the incredibly delicate indicator used on the original* Quest III. *One was fitted to each forestay about 6' above the deck. The four positions aft of the vane are for upwind sailing and the two at right angles for downwind.*

above: *This is the 1972 version of the Quest III wind indicator. One was mounted on a 3' high pedestal on each bow. Primitive but most effective.*

right: Weathercock *had this very simple little indicator mounted on the leading edge of her wing about 8' up.*

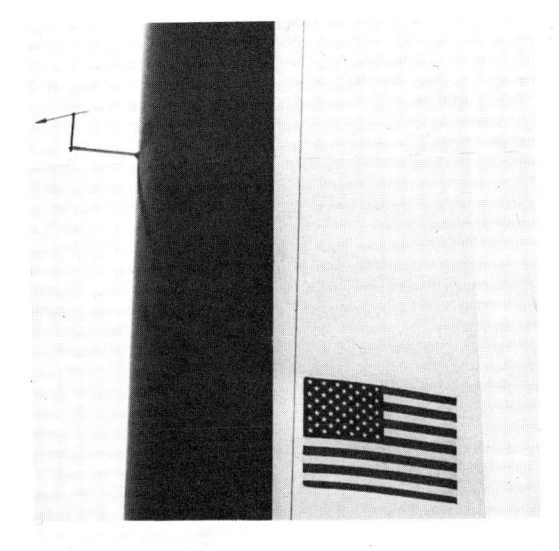

In this chapter we have attempted to summarize briefly some of the more important items of gear on a racing catamaran and hopefully the text and illustrations will encourage you to experiment with the equipment on your own boat, in search of that elusive small improvement. However, while on the subject of equipment, the importance of the personal gear and equipment worn or carried by the skipper and his crew must not be overlooked.

Both the skipper and the crew should always wear sailing shoes regardless of the weather conditions. A stubbed toe will almost certainly result in lost time. Besides, sailing shoes will enable the crew to move much more quickly and confidently around the boat in a crisis.

It should be the sole responsibility of the skipper to see that all the necessary gear is on board the boat before setting out for a race. The items we would normally carry for a race include the following:

Sailing instructions — including course.
International code flag guide.
Protest flag.
Combination tool — including shackle key, knife, screwdriver, spanner.
Spare shackles — large and small.
Piece of lashing — approximately three feet long.
Piece of cord — approximately ten feet long.
Yachting timer, watch or equivalent.
In hot weather — two cans of soft drink.
In cold weather — two bars of chocolate.

This is not an alarm clock to keep the crew awake in light weather but a very effective and inventive yacht timer. Simply a waterproofed kitchen clock with sweep second hand, it has been perfectly located on this Tornado where both skipper and crew can see it on either tack.

Obviously, you should have suitable wet weather clothing for your own particular racing conditions. In all but the tropical regions, a skin diver's wet suit is ideal for those colder days. It is a fact of life that the crew of a racing cat will get very wet, even in quite moderate winds and nothing is more detrimental to a boat's performance than crew who are feeling the cold.

And What of the Future?

Catamarans are certainly not just a passing fad — they are here to stay. They have found a permanent place in competitive small boat sailing and their future is assured.

But cats do not yet have universal acceptance. There are still many, many yachtsmen throughout the world who frown on them, and who are very ready to condemn them whenever they hear of one in trouble. They cannot (or will not) understand that first-class competitive yacht racing can be had in cats. Yet most of these critics have never sailed a cat let alone raced in one!

These attitudes are changing. Steadily, year by year, the opposition diminishes as more and more yachtsmen of all types and all ages develop a healthy respect for the main classes of racing catamaran. The respect is growing, too, for the skills and ability shown by those who sail and regularly race catamarans. The final step in the universal acceptance of the racing catamaran has been the inclusion of a cat class in the Olympic Games. We will see the Tornado in the 1976 Games in Canada and maybe the Australis or another monotype cat in 1980 or 1984. Catamarans have reached a stage in development that makes one thing certain. When the yachting classes are selected for every future Olympic Games, a catamaran must be one of the classes under consideration.

The growing universal acceptance of catamarans by small boat sailors and by small boat yacht clubs is extremely gratifying for those who have worked so hard for cats during the last ten or fifteen years. But it has also created its own special kind of problem which may not have an acceptable solution. This problem of the multiplicity of catamaran classes is especially prevalent in those countries and districts that have enjoyed cat sailing for a number of years. In Australia, in England and in the United States we have seen such a proliferation of catamaran classes of all shapes and sizes that good, keen and competitive racing has suffered.

In the countries that have taken on cats rather more recently, the problem has been avoided. These countries have had the advantage of learning by the mistakes of others. By supporting those classes that are already popular elsewhere, the international cat classes or classes that guarantee international racing opportunities, the number of different classes has been kept to a minimum.

In Australia there are over twenty active classes of racing catamaran. They vary in size from the smaller training classes of about eleven and a half feet up to the International C-class of twenty-five feet. Of course, not every class competes directly with another, but many do. For example, the size of the Australian Australis fleet is affected by a somewhat smaller following for the Unicorn, the locally designed Buccaneer and a smattering of Open A's. The largest class, numerically, in Australia is the sixteen-foot Cunningham designed mono-type, the Quickcat. This boat is wonderfully simple to build and offers fabulous one-design racing throughout the nation. But

145

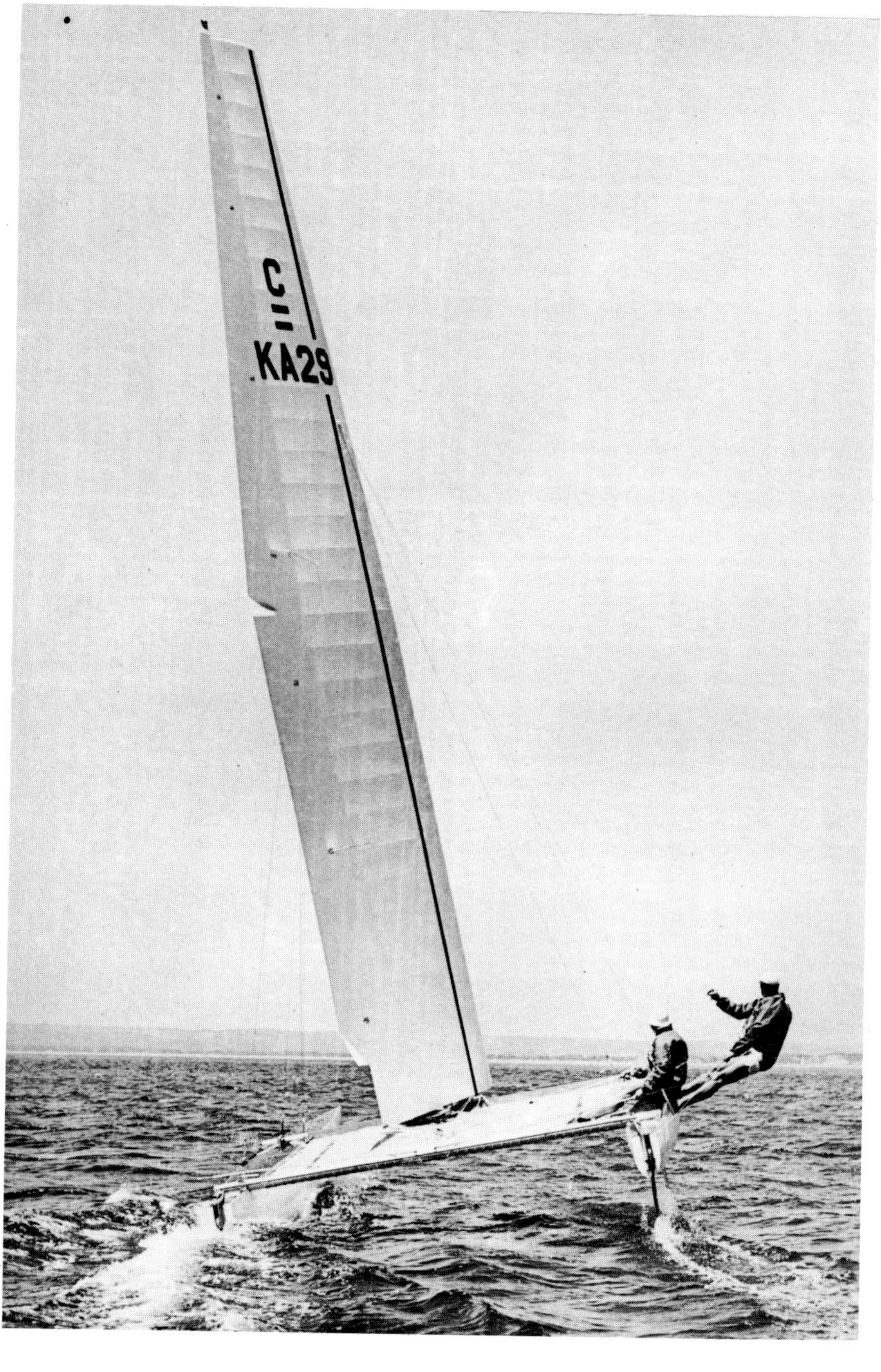
C
KA29

AND WHAT OF THE FUTURE?

because the class was designed some fifteen years ago, many believe it to be old-fashioned. So a number of newly designed classes of similar size have emerged. There are at least five other cat-rigged mono-type catamaran classes competing with the Quickcat, plus a couple of sloop-rigged ones. This ultimately means that the racing standard in each of these classes, including the Quickcat, must suffer. Fortunately for the Quickcat, it is still the strongest class numerically. It offers the best racing with fleets of nearly one hundred boats for championship events, and as a result the class continues to attract many of the top mono-type sailors.

Even the growth of the Tornado has been affected in some areas by a following for classes of similar size. In America, the B-Lion still has some support and enjoys regular fleet racing, and in Australia there is still a small pocket of open B's developed from the early Quest B. It is interesting to note that both these classes competed in the IYRU B-class selection trials and were soundly beaten by the Tornado. Our most senior yachting authority (the IYRU) can do no more to encourage the growth of international one-design classes.

What in effect we are saying is that the multitude of catamaran classes is bad for the standard of cat racing and bad for the orderly international growth of racing cats; yet we acknowledge and accept the role of progress. Without new designs and new classes we would have no new thought. And without this new thinking we cannot have progress.

There is little doubt that the future will see catamarans sailing even faster than

Left: There is no doubt that the total wing rig is here to stay for some time on International C-class — at least until it is perfected, or someone comes up with a rig even more efficient.

they do today. The existing classes will become more refined, more sophisticated and inevitably more complicated, and perhaps most significant of all, they will be better sailed. Catamarans today are attracting a much better standard of yachtsman than they did just a few years ago. With international competition in a number of classes, the tuning and sailing skills have greatly improved.

In spite of the large number of classes that are sailing today, new designs and new classes will continue to emerge. These will be lighter, stronger, more intricate and faster than the designs of today. Their rigs will be taller, more flexible, and have many more control systems. Some will have wing masts, even on small boats, and a few new designs will attempt to perfect the total wing rig.

One racing event, more than any other, generates by far the greatest amount of brilliant catamaran design output. This is, of course, the International Catamaran Challenge Trophy, now known everywhere as the Little America's Cup. While the Little America's Cup remains alive the design development will continue. We are not trying to suggest any waning interest in the Cup but only that the participating countries have a responsibility to keep the event very much alive and maintain the world-wide interest in it.

There has been much talk in recent years about the Little America's Cup event becoming a 'Round-Robin' series or even a conventional championship. There has even been talk of running the event along similar lines to the present America's Cup, whereby the defender can accept a number of simultaneous challenges, with the ultimate challenger being selected in a preliminary sail-off. Each of these ideas has its own group of devoted supporters and we cannot be certain which would be best for the long-term success of the event. If we were forced into a corner and

Handling of the wing rig will continue to be a problem and is perhaps the main reason why this type of rig will be confined to the developmental C-Class.

had to make a choice, we would favour the multi-country challenge with a preliminary selection series on the Cup course to select a challenger.

This system would seem to have two distinct advantages. The ultimate challenger would be at her peak of racing performance for the match, following the preliminary series. Under the present system this is often not the case as the challenger may have travelled from one hemisphere to another, from mid-winter to mid-summer, and have had five or six months without a race. It would also give the countries interested in C-class cats the opportunity of meeting on a regular basis to gain an accurate measure of their own comparative racing performance. The major disadvantage in this system is the very high cost for the challenging countries. For this reason we would favour the event being sailed under this system each alternate year and not annually as at present.

One other factor that may well influence the future of the Little America's Cup is the move by many leading helmsmen out of C-class into the International one-design classes such as the Tornado. For instance, the English cat sailors, who for many years pioneered international catamaran racing through the Little America's Cup, now put much of their serious racing efforts behind the Tornado. Men like Reg White, John Osborne and John Fisk are all totally dedicated to the Tornado. In fact, it is probably true that the fantastic success of the Tornado was

AND WHAT OF THE FUTURE?

a major contributing factor in the forced withdrawal of the English challenge for the 1973 Little America's Cup.

Spurred on by a desire to win the Little America's Cup, it is likely that the more significant and advanced design development for catamarans will continue to take place in the International C-class. In the last two years there has been a major breakthrough in rig design with the spectacular total wing rig. Unfortunately, the Danish experiment failed before any assessment could be made of the rig's potential. The American boat *Patient Lady II* also experienced major structural and control problems. However, the boat and more importantly the rig, did show great promise during the United States 1971 selection trials.

So far the Australian boat, *Miss Nylex*, has shown the best form of any C-class carrying a total wing sail rig. This boat was incredibly fast to windward in all winds except the very light, say below five miles per hour. Not only did she sail to windward much faster through the water, even than *Quest III*, but she also sailed closer to the wind. Unfortunately, her performance downwind was most erratic. Occasionally she did 'get in the groove' and sail very fast off the wind, proving perhaps that the potential is there. But her crew obviously experienced difficulty in understanding such a revolutionary rig and were unable to read the conditions well enough to make all the necessary adjustments during the races. *Miss Nylex* also experienced major boat-handling and control difficulties in winds over about twenty-three miles per hour. The rig was so efficient and so powerful that the boat was inclined to become an uncontrollable monster in fresher winds, especially downwind.

Maybe Roy Martin, the designer of *Miss Nylex*, can solve all these problems, or perhaps someone else will. One thing is certain, however, and that is that there will be many more total wing rigs developed for C-class cats in the search for greater efficiency and higher speeds.

Even the highly developed and efficient rig of *Quest III* has not reached its ultimate. Designer Lindsay Cunningham, soon after the 1972 defeat of the Americans, said that there were further things he could do to refine *Quest III*'s rig but that it might well require the use of exotic and highly expensive materials like titanium and carbon fibre.

As the steady refinement of these incredibly intricate C-class flyers continues, the boats and rigs will inevitably become more fragile. Not only will the rigs become more complex and susceptible to damage, but the hulls will be built lighter. Under the present rules of the Little America's Cup, these boats must race in winds up to thirty knots with a race only being cancelled if the wind is regularly gusting

The emergence of wing rigs on C-class cats will lead to experiments such as this on an Open B-class.

above this strength. It could well be argued, that any International class of sailing boat ought to be able to cope with winds of thirty knots for racing provided the waters were reasonably well sheltered. But does this general premise hold for International C-class and the Little America's Cup? Surely one of the prime objectives for this event is to further the advanced design of racing catamarans. With the vast sums of money and the great amount of time required to develop one of these boats, the risk of damage or destruction can be a deterrent to potential builders or designers.

Quest III has been thoroughly campaigned and tested over a number of years and has proved to be a very sound boat, but even she can experience severe handling difficulties and face the likelihood of serious damage in winds over about twenty-five miles per hour.

It is also becoming apparent that because these newer and more sophisticated rigs are so much heavier than the conventional aluminium mast and sail, the boats are not particularly happy in very light winds, especially if there is a sea running.

What we are predicting is a change in the rules for the Little America's Cup. If design development is to continue at an advanced rate but in a relatively orderly manner, the racing will need to be confined to winds between five and twenty-five knots. This will give the designers the freedom to concentrate on improving performance and efficiency without being restricted by the requirement to design a boat capable of withstanding those rare extreme conditions.

In the smaller and less spectacular classes of racing catamaran the design advances will continue. The B-class is, of course, now dominated by the International Tornado. And so it should be, for this was the reason for its selection by the IYRU late in 1967. In this instance the IRYU must be congratulated for making what has proved to be the correct decision. No doubt there will still be new designs developed in the basic 20 feet × 10 feet × 235 square feet category but it is most unlikely that any could seriously challenge the popularity of the Tornado in the immediate future. In Australia, there was a limited following for the Quest B, the Cunningham designed B-class which finished second to the Tornado in the selection trials. And it is true to say that the very best of these boats, particularly when sailed by Bruce Proctor, was often able to beat a good Tornado in light to moderate breezes. However, the steady growth of the Tornado in Australia (nearly one hundred boats in 1972), the Olympic status and the very strict one-design rules have obviously appealed to many cat sailors and the interest in the Quest B has waned to a stage where they no longer enjoy fleet racing. The B-Lion story is similar but this class does still have a following in North America.

We feel sure that every cat sailor in the world was thrilled to see the Tornado as an Olympic class. Not because they sail a Tornado, or ever want to sail one — in fact, they may not even like the Tornado — but because the Tornado's selection is true recognition for *all* catamarans in the world today. The Tornado certainly meets all the demanding requirements of an international one-design class. The Tornado will continue to grow and to dominate the competitive international catamaran racing. The class is already attracting yachtsmen from other classes, mono-hulls included, and many of these were in world class before making the change. The rules of the Tornado are basically excellent and the class administration is competent and efficient.

There should be little need to make

AND WHAT OF THE FUTURE? 151

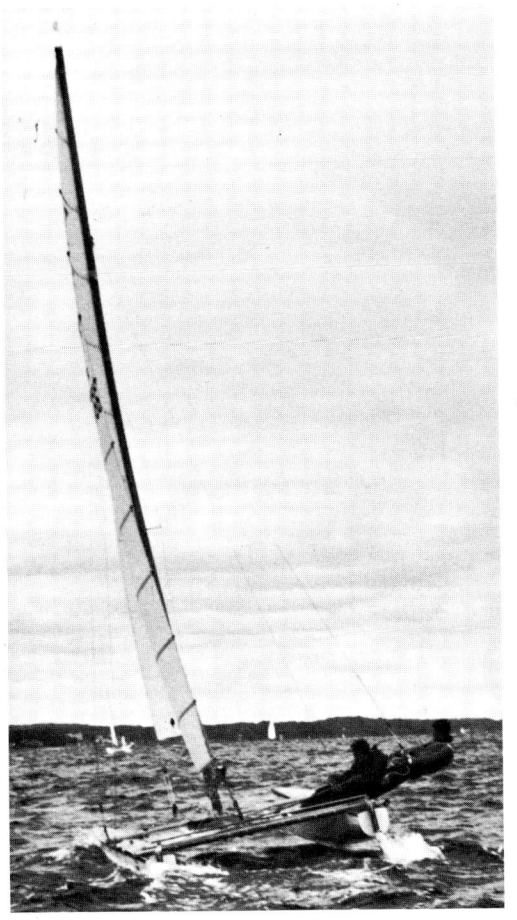

The Tornado has proved to be an ideal International one-design racing class. Her class administration is efficient and the class rules well conceived. We believe that the future will see a minor change in the class rules to allow a diamond stay system that can be adjusted while sailing, preferably while racing. The severe bend in this mast of Reg White in these two pictures, highlights the problem of having to set up the rig in conditions that might differ from those experienced during a race.

changes to the Tornado rules in the near future, with a couple of possible exceptions. At the moment the only rigging permitted on the mast, apart from the usual side stays and forestay, is a set of diamond stays rigged below the hounds. These diamonds certainly do the job in stiffening the mast and allowing it to bend within predetermined limits. However, the rules do not permit their tension to be adjusted during a race. In fact, the rules are so worded as to make it almost impossible to adjust the tension while on the water before a race. In other words,

In an attempt to gain even more control over sail shape, this Tornado was set up with wires leading from the end of each batten, on both sides of the sail, down the mast to a control system. Apart from it being contrary to class rules, it proved too complex to be effective.

it means that the diamond tension must be pre-set on the shore before a race and not changed until the boat comes ashore. This can be quite restrictive in tuning the boat for the prevailing conditions, especially in Europe where it is quite common for two races to be sailed in rapid succession without the fleet returning to shore.

We have found that the diamond tension in the Tornado has a great influence over the tune of the rig and does require adjustment for different wind and sea conditions. We believe that one day a simple rigging adjuster that can be adjusted while racing will be permitted, and that the class will be even more competitive if this comes about.

The growth of the A-class has so far been quite different from the B-class. Although back in 1967 the IYRU did select a one-design class, the Australian-designed Australis, it did not immediately enjoy a burst of enthusiastic support at the expense of the other A designs. It is true that it did take some time to get the final drawings, class rules and building method for the Australis finalized and this may have hampered the growth of this class. But even before this, it became apparent that there was a following for some of the other classes in the selection trials. The Unicorn had a solid core of supporters and these were growing in spite of the IYRU decision. The A-Lion was in a similar situation. Meanwhile the Australis had solved the early problems and was becoming established as an international class. But strangely enough there were still new designs appearing within this A classification, and this trend has continued.

Fortunately, the Australis has now become well established in international yachting but still has a little way to go to catch the Tornado. It is also quite obvious that the Australis will not meet the needs of all the yachtsmen who wish to race cats of the A-class size. We believe that this will always be the case. It will make it a little more difficult for the Australis but there is room for both the International Australis and an open A-class. Of the high performance cats, the A-class is the lowest in cost and does represent the best opportunity for individuals to experiment with their own design ideas. As long as there are racing sailing boats there will always be people not particularly interested in one-design racing but more inclined to create their own designs. We

AND WHAT OF THE FUTURE?

believe that the A-class is the right class for this and that the IYRU should consider formally recognizing the 'International Open A-class Catamaran'. In saying this, we stress that this should not in any way effect the continued IYRU support for the one-design Australis.

Every country has its own special peculiarities and we have already mentioned that Australia has well over twenty different catamaran classes. Many of these classes are really unnecessary but not so with them all. In Australia, with its vast distances, most small sailing boats are kept at the owner's home on a trailer and towed to the water for each day's racing. The maximum width allowed on Australian roads is eight feet.

We feel that this limitation has slowed the growth of the Tornado and has certainly encouraged the development of three other classes. Each of these meets the same basic measurement requirements of eighteen feet long with eight-foot beam, approximately two hundred and fifteen square feet sail area and a two-man crew. These broad measurement guidelines were drawn up by an enthusiastic group of Sydney cat sailors many years ago, before the creation of the Tornado. At that time they believed a boat meeting these requirements would be ideal for their weekend racing.

Many designs were developed by this group but none were quite right. But after a season or two the standard of their new boats was improving until eventually the rather pretty and quite popular Stingray class was evolved. Following close on the heels (or is it sterns?) of the Stingray came the similar-sized Black Witch class which has an unmistakable resemblance to the Tornado. And now, in the last twelve months, we have seen another class also of this same basic size, called the QB 2. This most recent class is a Cunningham creation with hulls of the well-established Quest shape. Incidentally, this catamaran size category has created for itself the all-embracing description of 'B2-class'.

B2 is not one of the catamaran divisions set down by the IYRU nor is it officially recognized by any national yachting authority as a class. But the lack of official

The Australian designed and developed Stingray class could well find a place in the international catamaran racing world. The boat is 18' long with 8' beam. Both skipper and crew use a trapeze. Certainly there seems to be a need for a cat class of these basic dimensions in countries where 8' is the maximum width allowed on the road.

recognition has not adversely affected the growth of these three classes. Obviously there is a demand for this size of cat, and as the Tornado grows in popularity and status these slightly smaller classes will provide valuable training for Tornado aspirants. We believe that this size of cat could well have appeal in other countries, particularly the Stingray which is an extremely well-conceived and developed high-performance racing cat.

It is likely, too, that the growth will continue in the smaller training classes of cat. Already these smaller cats are very popular in Australia and we feel that when the youngsters in other countries discover the fabulous fun that can be had in these little catamarans, their growth will extend across the world. The most popular training cat in Australia is the Arafura Cadet. This is an eleven-foot plywood cat carrying a sloop rig. It is sailed either by two young children, of say eight to ten years of age, or by one older child. In fact, they do sail very efficiently with one lightly-built adult. The Arafura Cadet is available in kit form and is extremely easy to assemble. You might even call the Arafura the Mirror Dinghy of catamarans.

There are also a couple of other high-performance cats in this smaller category that are worth watching for future international growth potential. There is the Australian-designed Arrow, a fourteen-foot version of the Arafura but far more sophisticated. This class is raced throughout Australia as a mono-type using trapeze. They sail incredibly fast for their size and are far more manageable than the larger cats of A-class size. They can be car-topped. The other fourteen-footer that is rapidly attracting top skippers is the cat-rigged mono-type, the Paper Tiger. The Paper Tiger originated in New Zealand, and quickly became popular in Australia. There is now a growing interest

The boat in the foreground is the fabulous little training class, the Arafura Cadet. Only 11' 6" long, this plywood cat is very easy to build from a kit and can be sailed either by two children or one larger child or adult. Boat 118 behind is her larger sister, the 14' Arrow, a trapeze-equipped monotype. We believe that junior cat classes such as these will soon become popular internationally with young people.

in the class outside these two southern countries. It looks very smart and is an extremely manageable little racing catamaran.

The Hobie Cat is, of course, an incredible success story. The Hobie 14 has become popular world wide and now we are seeing the sixteen-foot sloop-rigged Hobie also enjoy immediate success. The Hobie 14 is so simple and so free of

AND WHAT OF THE FUTURE?

maintenance that it is almost unbelievable. It is also superbly well engineered and sturdily built. It has to be, to take the pounding in the surf on the US west coast. Compared with other cats of similar size, the Hobie is relatively expensive. We must confess that when we first saw the Hobie and the price tag we did not predict a future for this class outside America, but we were so wrong. This only goes to prove that you should never judge any sailing boat solely by your own personal requirements in a boat. The success of the Hobie has shown that there are a group of cat sailors who have neither the time, inclination nor ability to build or equip their own cat. They prefer to buy one 'off the shelf'. We believe that the Hobie is good for the catamaran movement in that it introduces new sailors to catamarans — a few Hobie sailors have already moved into the more serious and sophisticated classes.

Before concluding our brief look into the future of catamaran racing, we thought we might devote some space to a discussion of the perfect racing course for cats. Perhaps the perfect racing course will never be found but in recent years the IYRU and race committees throughout the world have devoted many hours to finding the ideal solution.

In setting a course for catamarans the race committee must realize that there are a number of special requirements. Because of a catamaran's greater speed, the total length of the course must be considerably longer than a course for a mono-hull dinghy of similar size. In a fifteen-to twenty-knot breeze a normal cat race should last anything from a minimum of one and a half hours to, say, a maximum of two and a quarter hours. This means a total course length of eighteen to twenty miles for a C-class race and fifteen to eighteen miles for an A-class or Tornado. If a conventional Olympic course of triangle, windward-return, windward is set, the legs of the course will be very long indeed making the marks extremely difficult to see and the race somewhat dreary.

The Olympic course can readily be extended by adding another triangle or another windward-return, or both.

In fact, the course used for the 1972 Little America's Cup off Sorrento Sailing Club near Melbourne was what we might term the double Olympic course. It consisted of a triangle, windward-return, triangle, windward-return and a windward leg to the finish. The windward legs were approximately one and three-quarters miles in length. The first reach, which was roughly at right-angles to the wind, was approximately one and a half miles, and the broad reach was approximately two and a quarter miles. This gave a total course length of just under twenty miles which proved to be perfect for an event such as this.

This course can be further analysed as follows:

Upwind —
  5 windward legs   8·75 miles
Downwind —
  2 leads   3·0 miles
  2 broad reaches 4·5 ,,
  2 square runs   3·5 ,,
                          11·00 miles

                          19·75 miles

We believe that this is close to the perfect blend of upwind sailing, reaching and running for catamaran racing. For smaller classes, such as the Tornado or even the Australis, the windward leg can be reduced to one and a half miles, the tight reach to one and a quarter miles and the broad reach to just under two miles. This gives a total course length of about sixteen and a half miles, which is still a good length course — perhaps a little too

Already the Hobie 14 has astounded its critics in achieving such rapid growth. The newer two-man Hobie 16 is likely to gain a similar following.

AND WHAT OF THE FUTURE?

Hydrofoils have been tried before on catamarans and they will most likely be tried again. But they have yet to prove successful. This Australian hydrofoil equipped C-class designed by Bob Miller (who also designed the Contender) never got off the ground.

long for week by week club racing, but certainly essential for championship events.

If a course of less than sixteen miles is required we would strongly recommend against shortening the windward leg below one and a half miles. This can be achieved by dropping either one of the triangles or one of the windward-returns.

We know that the International Tornado Association, in conjunction with the IYRU, has developed a course which it believes to be more suited to Tornados and the other high-performance cats. This course has as its basic triangle a windward leg of 2·5 km (1·55 miles), a right-angle reaching leg of 3·0 km (1·86 miles) and a broad reach of approximately 3·9 km (2·42 miles). There has already been some criticism of this course and it does seem to place undue emphasis on the downwind part of the race. This comment applies particularly to the lead or tight reach, the least tactical leg of any racing course.

We would like to suggest another type of course that might be worth a try by some adventurous catamaran race committee. Unfortunately, there is a small complication in that it requires the normal three marks, windward, leeward and wing, plus an additional wing mark. The course is best described in a diagram, but basically it calls for three complete rounds of the course plus a windward leg to finish. The course can be described thus:

Round 1: Triangle, with the right-angle at the windward mark.
Round 2: Windward and return.
Round 3: Triangle with the right-angle at the wing mark.
Round 4: Windward to finish.

The dual wing mark problem can be handled in two ways. The wing mark could be laid for the first triangle, picked up and moved during the windward-return, laid in the new position for the final triangle. The committee boat having the task of moving the mark could also act

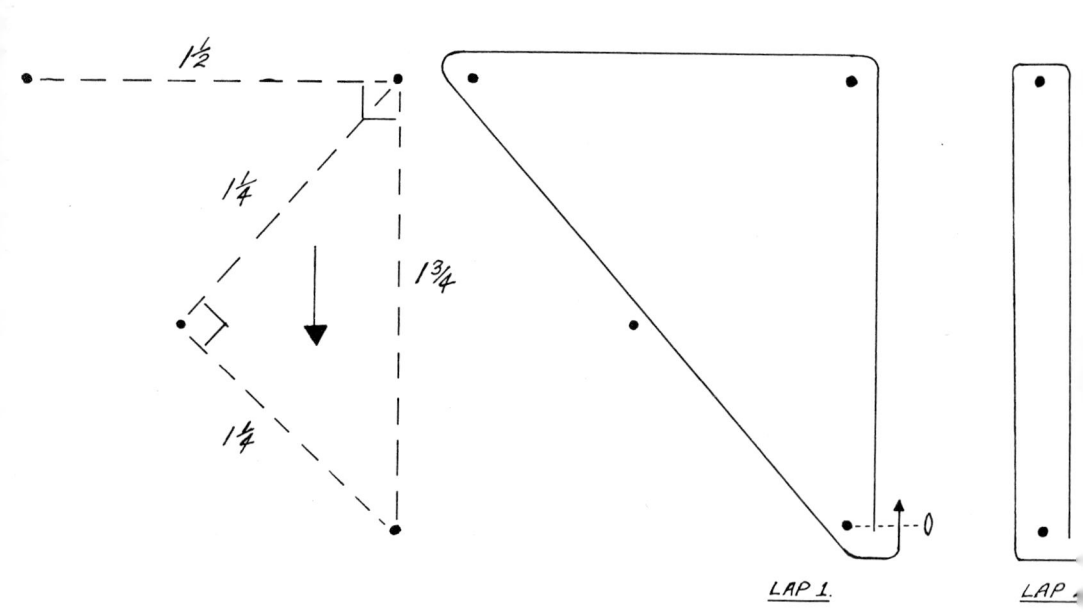

This experimental course for catamarans has some advantages in that it does provide racing on five different points of sailing. Two wing marks could be laid, or the mark moved after the fleet has completed the first round.

as a marker boat. The other alternative would be for both marks to be laid at the one time and left in position for the whole race. Again a mark boat would greatly assist in identification.

If this course is laid with a windward leg of one and three-quarter miles, a lead of one and a half miles, a broad reach of two and a quarter miles, and the two beam reaches of one and a quarter miles each, it gives a total of fifteen miles. This course has many advantages in that it offers some racing on each of five different types of leg. It could work well for cats and the

AND WHAT OF THE FUTURE?

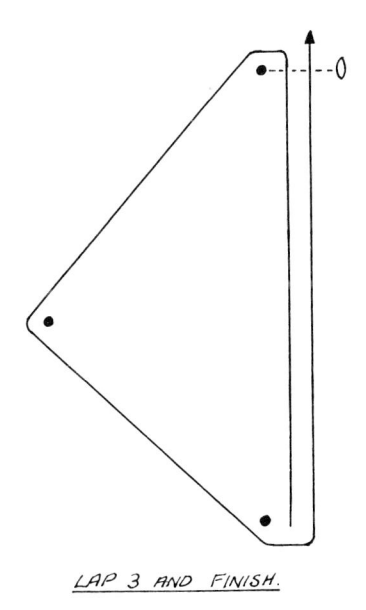

LAP 3 AND FINISH.

two wing marks would not create too much of a problem, especially after the skippers had sailed the course once or twice. We would like to see a fleet try this course for a championship series, provided there is an invitation race or two before the heats begin, and let us know how it works out.